THE SIDE DOOR

WELCOMING GOD'S DIVINE DETOURS

CINDY LAFAVRE YORKS

All Scripture quotations, unless otherwise indicated, are taken from the Holy Bible, New International Version®, NIV®. Copyright © 1973, 1978, 1984, 2011 by Biblica, Inc.™ Used by permission of Zondervan. All rights reserved worldwide. www.zondervan.com The "NIV" and "New International Version" are trademarks registered in the United States Patent and Trademark Office by Biblica, Inc.™

Scriptures marked (ESV) are from The ESV® Bible (The Holy Bible, English Standard Version®), copyright © 2001 by Crossway, a publishing ministry of Good News Publishers. Used by permission. All rights reserved.

Scriptures marked (NLT) are taken from the Holy Bible, New Living Translation, copyright ©1996, 2004, 2015 by Tyndale House Foundation. Used by permission of Tyndale House Publishers, Inc., Carol Stream, Illinois 60188. All rights reserved.

Scriptures marked (NASB) taken from the NEW AMERICAN STANDARD BIBLE®, Copyright © 1960, 1962, 1963, 1968, 1971, 1972, 1973, 1975, 1977, 1995 by The Lockman Foundation. Used by permission.

Scriptures marked (MSG) are taken from The Message. Copyright © 1993, 1994, 1995, 1996, 2000, 2001, 2002. Used by permission of NavPress Publishing Group.

Printed in the United States of America.

ISBN: 978-0-9980481-0-9

TABLE OF CONTENTS

WEEK 1: THE SIDE DOOR

WEEK 2 : THANKING GOD

WEEK 3: DISTANCE FROM GOD

WEEK 4: CULTURAL CAMOUFLAGE

WEEK 5: TESTING 1, 2, 3

WEEK 6: CONSISTENCY

WEEK 7: CURTAIN CALL

WEEK 8: THE CROSS

WEEK 9: UNWRAPPING PRESENT MOMENT GIFTS

WEEK 10: LOVE

WEEK 1: THE SIDE DOOR

THE SIDE DOOR: UNEXPECTED ACCESS

My friend Heather was deep in the throes of a home remodel. Usually optimistic and upbeat, she had been under severe stress for months. Every room of her small home was in complete disarray due to several do-it-yourself remodeling projects. Belongings, clothes, and possessions were in heaps and piles in every room as she waited for half-done projects to be completed. Finally, she realized she was completely overwhelmed. She broke down crying and called a friend to come over for support and encouragement.

Heather's friend examined the mess and suggested a solution to Heather's clutter problem: gather non-essentials and stash them in a trailer parked outside. That way there would be less stuff in each room, and after the remodeling was complete, Heather could replace everything needed in the proper spot.

After the items to be stored were gathered, the two of them proceeded to the front door of the trailer with the stuff. But there were too many items to shove in the front of the space, no matter what angle they tried or the method they used to try to cram it in. Heather's friend suggested they try the door on the side of the trailer. Sure enough, everything fit perfectly. The clutter was removed, and a small measure of peace was restored as she and her hubby wrapped up their remodel.

God often takes His people through a side door to accomplish His purposes. Moses entered palatial Egyptian living through a side door via a basket floating down the Nile River. God's people spent decades in purgatory after entering the "side door" of the desert, waiting to inhabit the Promised Land. Joseph was sold into slavery before becoming second to the Egyptian king in power and authority. Jesus Christ was born into this world through the side door of mortal birth.

The side door isn't always the most heralded. It is rarely the most appealing. It's not our "go-to" entrance. We feel more deserving of the front door, put off by the side door's unpretentious status. Our journey may have unexpected turns and potholes, but sometimes God takes us by the hand and leads us through it. He wants us to trust Him to lead us to the forks in the road best able to refine us as He sees fit.

Keys to Kingdom Living: When God is our GPS, we will end up at His destination.

Doorpost: "But He commanded the skies to open; He opened the doors of heaven. He rained down manna for them to eat; He gave them bread from heaven." Psalm 78:23–24

THE SIDE DOOR: THE HUMBLE ENTRANCE

*C*elebrity images fill the screens of iPads, phones, and TVs throughout our star-struck land. The voracious appetite for glamorous images of svelte young women gliding down the red carpet cannot be satiated. After their 15 minutes of fame and countless photo ops, they make their grand entrance through the front doors of their designated VIP venue.

Dignitaries and VIP's have been making their grand entrances for years—the powerful king, the zealous politician, the blushing bride. These people never enter through a side door. That entrance is traditionally reserved for "the help." In palatial settings and even grand hotels, we usually see Service Only doors and elevators. In a famous scene from *Gone with the Wind*," the beautiful Scarlett O'Hara descends from a grand staircase to a love-struck Rhett Butler.

But the most important entrance into the world in the history of the world did not occur with great fanfare. Our Messiah, the Savior of the world, the Son of God was born of a woman. He did not enter into the world to live in a marble palace rife with gold filigree. His first breath was drawn in a humble stable. He entered into the world His Father created through the side door—God as man, in the form of a helpless baby. He was laid, not on a crib with 600 thread count sheets, but on a bed of straw in a crude manger. He did not command the grand entrance He was more than worthy of receiving. God tells us in His Word that His ways are not our ways. This truth plays out not only in the life of His Son but in ours as well.

The side door through which Jesus entered the world as a servant was not the door the Jewish people envisioned their Messiah would use. But He came to save, not to conquer. In John 10:9 He said, "I am the door." Jesus will again return in all His glory. He will return with all the fanfare suited to the King of Kings and Lord of Lords. In Matthew 23:12, He told His disciples, "He who humbles himself will be exalted." The other half of that verse says he who exalts himself will be humbled. Sometimes a trip through a side door is just what we need, even if it isn't always what we want.

Keys to Kingdom Living: Be humble and flexible, and cultivate a servant's heart through humility and obedience to God as you walk down unexpected paths.

Doorpost: "He guides the humble in what is right and teaches them His way." Psalm 25:9

THE SIDE DOOR: WHERE GOD KNOCKS

*I*t doesn't take a genius to see how Americans are marketed to and seduced into consumption. When you wake up and check your phone, there are most likely emails crowding your inbox about today's myriad of online sales. Turn on morning TV and you may be tempted by ads for sizzling bacon, sugary coffees, and restaurant breakfasts large enough to feed your entire block. Billboards, mail-order catalogs, and street signage all compete for allegiance and dollars. Yet consumers possess the free will to choose what to purchase, what to eat, what to refuse or embrace.

Free will has been a nemesis and a godsend since Eve bit into the forbidden fruit. God's design incorporated our right to choose then—and still does today. Before sin entered the picture, there were no doors between God and men. But when Adam and Eve broke with God due to their poor choices, God ushered them out of the garden and essentially closed the door to Eden.

Without free will, we are slaves to whatever we are bound to. In the dictionary, the opposite of free will is subjugation, which is to "bring under domination or control by conquest." God doesn't want robots; He could have made legions of beings in any state He chose. God wants true followers who freely choose to belong to Him, delight in His will, and walk in His ways (Psalm 119:47).

Some people view rules as a drag and a hindrance to their fun. Yet in Galatians 2, Paul tells us there is "freedom in the law" because we are free from the bondage of sin as we live by faith and enjoy God's grace. When we embrace or say yes to things that are not good for us, we are bound by, and to, them. This principle is at the root of addictions of all kinds: substance abuse, alcoholism, overeating, and sexual addiction. It also points to the poor choices made when people put their trust in idols of their own making: success, fame, or even good things that can take over our lives, like caring for children, attention to a spouse, or even emphasizing pastors above their messages.

God tells us in His Word that He wants "everyone to come to repentance" (2 Peter 3:9). But we have to let Him into our hearts and claim the salvation purchased by the blood of the Lamb. We must choose Jesus Christ! In Revelation, our Lord Jesus says this: "I stand at the door and knock" —but we must open it! To the one who is victorious, the one who chooses life in abundance and does not refuse the invitation, he will be given the right to sit with Him—Jesus—on His throne. This God-designed seating arrangement cannot be earned; it must be chosen. The question is, will we answer God's call at our side door? Will we enter into a life devoted to Him with an undivided heart?

Keys to Kingdom Living: Don't think twice about answering God's call on your life.

Doorpost: "I stand at the door and knock. If anyone hears my voice and opens the door, I will come in and eat with that person, and they with me." Revelation 3:20

THE SIDE DOOR: WHERE YOU LET GOD IN

*H*ave you ever had a door slammed in your face, or been refused entrance to somewhere you wanted to be or go? I can recall several instances when I was denied access to my desired destinations. Once, on a visit to Paris, an elegant boutique limited the number of people allowed inside on a day. Unfortunately, because it was so close to closing time, the limit was reached so waiting would have done no good. I never was able to return there on my trip. Access denied.

Back in the '80s, when I was a young reporter, I traveled to New York to attend the seasonal shows of the most prominent American fashion designers. Tickets to these shows were sometimes difficult to obtain, and many of my colleagues were refused entrance if they were not from a prestigious, big-city newspaper. When actress/singer Cher came out with a designer fragrance, the splashy fragrance launch happened to coincide with her birthday. Reporters scrambled for invitations to this posh event commemorating the occasion. Though I was from Los Angeles, I worked for the secondary newspaper at the time and did not make the list. Fortunately, good friends got me into the party and I was able to cover it for my newspaper. But had I not secured the coveted ticket, I would have been out in the cold —literally!—and in the doghouse at work.

Jesus Christ came to earth to save, but many continue to

refuse Him entrance into their hearts. Imagine the pain of this rejection, considering the unimaginable suffering and the price He paid with His very life. Many people—including some we know and love—are regularly exposed to Him. They may have grown up around believers or have been exposed to His Word on a steady basis. Perhaps they are surrounded by caring friends and loved ones trying to bring them to Jesus. The only thing that stands in the way of their salvation is their willingness to open themselves up to what is behind the door. And, at the end of the day, no matter how many people lead them to the door, they have to be the ones willing to knock and allow Jesus to open the door for them and lead them to eternal life.

Jesus never denies anyone entry to this door. He has no A-list —He is all-inclusive. He doesn't care if you are from a town of a hundred people or a city of six million. Access isn't dependent on others to get you in. You don't need the right clothes or money, prestige or success. What you do need is a heart that is willing and a spirit that is humble enough to do your best to obey God. He tells us in Matthew 7:21, "Not everyone . . . will enter the kingdom of heaven, but only the one who does the will of my Father." Are you willing to let the door swing open to life in abundance?

Keys to Kingdom Living: Open your heart and mind, then open the door.

Doorpost: "Ask and it will be given to you; seek and you will find; knock and the door will be opened to you." Matthew 7:7

THE SIDE DOOR: THE CLOSED DOOR
THAT KEEPS THE GARBAGE OUT

*I*n our world of specialized services, the art of the stylish closet has become a thriving industry. Today, many closets are featured on lifestyle TV shows. Jewelry, shoes, and purses line the shelves. Of course, like so many things we see on TV, these are hardly images of the average closet. Many people—including me—have closets cluttered enough to cause embarrassment if anyone tried to open them.

When my son was little and I asked him to clean his room, he would shove everything in his bedroom closet (clean or dirty!) and hope I wouldn't open that door to see his deceptive attempt at tidying his space. Hoarders who have trouble distinguishing what needs to be kept and what needs to be thrown away sometimes stuff their closets with unnecessary items—even garbage. The task of cleaning out the closet is one often left at the bottom of many a to-do list because of its tedious nature.

One way to keep this dilemma at bay is to be discerning about what goes into the closet in the first place. If we resist holding onto garbage, that space remains clean and uncluttered, ready for what it was designed to do: to house the stuff we *want* to hold onto.

The closet of our minds works in much the same way. When we are transformed by the renewing of our minds, as Paul says in Romans 12:2, we are to deliberately choose non-conformity in our world. We should be careful what we let pass before our eyes, enter our minds, and pass through our ears. We need to keep the door shut on certain things in our troubled world, for our own minds, but especially for the minds of our children. If garbage begins to take over wherever it is laid, it eventually monopolizes that space. It can even take on a life of its own and spawn new life; anyone who has ever found a moldy apple core or the too-old cheese in the fridge knows what I'm talking about.

We need to remove the garbage from our soul too. Nobody knew that better than David. He went before God and asked Him to "examine . . . test . . . search" his heart and mind as he asked for His mercy. We need to do that, too. We need to remove the garbage of wrongdoing, disobedience, and even seemingly benign missteps such as not helping out a friend or missing an opportunity to serve God. He already sees and knows about the garbage in our closets. No door can keep Him from doing that. In fact, God told Ezekiel to dig through a wall and peek through a doorway. In chapter 8 of his book in the Bible, Ezekiel was told to "see the evil and abominations" being done there. God says the people think He can't see them. But our all-seeing, all-knowing God's view is never obstructed. Are we willing to clean?

Keys to Kingdom Living: Take out the garbage in your mind, heart, and soul.

Doorpost: "Do not conform to the pattern of this world, but be transformed by the renewing of your mind." Romans 12:2

THE SIDE DOOR: WHERE INTRUDERS MAY ATTEMPT ENTRY

*I*n quaint small towns, some citizens boast how they never lock their doors. Whether their judgment is sound or naïve, they base their decision on their feeling that they are safe and do not need the protection of a lock. Today's lifestyles seem to require a barrage of locks: a padlock for the locker at the gym or your bike, a LoJack system for the car, both a deadbolt and standard lock for the door of your home, and passcode locks for iPads and cell phones.

In this day and age, it's probably wise to lock the doors of your home. The newspapers are filled with story after story about burglaries, robberies, and tales of people trying to break into homes and cars to steal things. But some doors are more fortified than others, and some may require more vigilance to secure. A lock is only effective if it's properly used.

The Enemy would like nothing more than to rob you of your joy and peace. God, of course, supplies "the peace that passes all understanding" (Phil. 4:7) and invites us to enter His gates with thanksgiving and praise and the joy that experience brings (Psalm 100:4). The Enemy waits for opportunities to prey on those unprepared for his attacks. Sometimes they are overt. Other times they are subtle, and before we know it, we have stumbled. We must plan our defense *before* the attack is made.

If you leave your door of resolve open, the Enemy will

"break in and steal" (Matthew 6:19) before you realize it. If we don't guard our hearts, we are vulnerable to all kinds of sabotage: depression, hopelessness, violence, even criminal wrongdoing. But if you secure your "door" and resolve to prevent the Enemy from getting in, you will have prevented that opportunity from happening. We need to "set our minds on things above, not on earthly things" (Colossians 3:2). In 2 Corinthians 2:11 (The Message), Paul cautions against giving "Satan an opening for yet more mischief—we are not oblivious to his sly ways."

We may not be oblivious—but we are not always on guard, either. We need God to put His armor on us every day: the belt of truth, the breastplate of righteousness, the shield of faith, the helmet of salvation, and the sword of the Spirit" (Ephesians 6:11). If we take the time and effort to submit ourselves to God's protection, we will be able to "extinguish all the flaming arrows of the evil one" (Ephesians 6:16). Going out without our armor is the spiritual equivalent of leaving the house in our underwear. We must protect ourselves by keeping a tight rein on the good and actively seeking God's protection as a blockade to keep out the rest.

Keys to Kingdom Living: Keep your door locked and wear your armor of God so you can fight off temptation and make godly choices.

Doorpost: "The thief comes only to steal and kill and destroy; I have come that they may have life, and have it to the full." John 10:10

THE SIDE DOOR: WHERE OTHERS KNOCK

*W*e've all had that moment when the inconvenient phone call, the knock at the door, or the tap on the shoulder in the middle of that hurried errand interrupts us—when the last thing we have time for is a 20-minute discussion with anyone. And yet there is a need: a friend requires a shoulder, or a listening ear, or maybe even some sound advice. In our minds, we think we are helpful, but often we want to "help" on our own terms. We are willing to go the extra mile . . . as long as it coincides with our own schedule.

Looking at these missed opportunities on the outside and not acting on them does not necessarily constitute sinful behavior. Sometimes we really do have a dentist appointment or a pressing engagement we must keep. But what if someone is in need of help and we simply won't bother to take the time when we could? How does that stand up to Jesus's commandment of "love one another as I have loved you" (John 15:12)?

We learn in God's Word that Jesus is the door. But many people in your life have yet to go through that door. People who don't know Jesus might need someone like you to lead them there. If they aren't of the presence of mind to knock at His door yet, they might first knock at yours. Once they have come to you for help or wise counsel, you can lead them to Jesus. Are we willing to give till it hurts, the way Jesus did? You've probably heard that expression, "Jesus with skin on." This is what Christians are to the unsaved. The unsaved are able to catch sight of salvation through the side door of relationship with a Christ-follower who genuinely cares. The Christian who reaches out doesn't just care enough to help meet an immediate need: they care enough to help lead those with the *greatest* unmet need to The Door, Christ Himself.

Sometimes knocks are less direct. We may perceive a need while reading the mail or seeing an ad on TV. Acting on these leads requires commitment and perseverance. We may sacrifice time, energy, and comfort. It might be more fun to go shopping at the mall to buy expensive gifts for your family than to spend time and money providing a Christmas celebration for a poor Mexican village. But that is exactly the kind of thing God calls us to do. In Matthew 6:19, Jesus says, "Do not store up riches for yourselves here on earth." There is a famous line in the '80s movie *Wall Street* where Martin Sheen asks Michael Douglas, "How many yachts can you water ski behind? How much is enough?"

Are we truly willing to live by Jesus's first and greatest commandment? We may not perfect the art of living, but we can aspire to it.

Keys to Kingdom Living: Remain flexible enough to bend over backwards for others instead of insisting on standing up for what you want or need at all costs.

Doorpost: "For I was hungry and you gave me food, I was thirsty and you gave me drink, I was a stranger and you welcomed me . . . Truly, I say to you, as you did it to one of the least of these my brothers, you did it to me." Matthew 25:35, 40 (ESV)

WEEK 2 : THANKING GOD

THANKING GOD IN MY PAIN

*I*t's easy to be thankful when Hallmark commercials littered with pumpkins play nonstop. But what if you can't make the rent? Or you're worried about stretching your food stamps until the end of the month? Or despairing over when the next midnight phone call might come from jail where a loved one is locked up after making yet another poor choice? The truth is, being thankful in all circumstances is where the rubber really does meet the road in the journey of the Christian life.

There are three reasons why we are to be truly thankful even when we don't feel it. The first reason: When we emanate thankfulness, we take a worrying focus off of ourselves, retool that worry into trust, and lean on God. His promises are rich in truth: "God will meet all your needs according to the riches of His glory in Christ Jesus." (Philippians 4:19). Some people misinterpret this passage, imagining all our *wants* will be met—when, instead, our salvation meets our truest and deepest *need*: redemption from the Pit. We need to be truly thankful for this greatest gift, at all times and in all places.

An important aspect of cultivating a thankful heart: God doesn't expect us to be thankful *about* our circumstances. We don't have to fall to bended knee when husbands walk out or children stumble down the wrong path. God knows our pain and wants us to cry out to Him in raw honesty. There is nothing more off-putting to others and even to God than inauthenticity. Jeremiah, Job, and Habakkuk, all devoted men of God—each cried out to God in utter despair. But it was David, one of the most eloquent scribes of the Bible, who laid out his laments in psalm after psalm, laying bare his very soul. Feeling abandoned by God, as we often do in our pain, he writes in Psalm 22 the famous words uttered later on the cross by Jesus Himself: "My God, my God, why have you forsaken me? Why are you so far from saving me in the words of my groaning?"

We often wonder why we're in pain, and we might not always understand the purpose for our trials, even though the truth is that God is close to the brokenhearted (Psalm 34:18). He promises to "save those who are crushed in spirit." The trap some of us fall into is in trying to foist our timetable onto God's plans.

But the second reason we are to be thankful in all circumstances is because people are watching how we handle grief and disappointment. Fellow Christians find inspiration in a godly example of authentic suffering—especially when it is followed by perseverance. Non-Christians observe how suffering believers allow God into their pain and problems. This curiosity can lead to a conversation about "the hope we have."

The final reason we're to be thankful no matter what: it's God's command.

Keys to Kingdom Living: Cry out honestly to God but remain thankful for all He's done.

Doorpost: "Give thanks in all circumstances, for this is God's will for you in Christ Jesus." 1 Thessalonians 5:18

THANKING GOD IN ADVANCE

I remember the first time someone thanked God in advance for what He was going to do: they were praying over me about a crucial fork in my road. My first thought was, wow, this is awesome, and it really feels like a done deal. Sometimes in our prayer life when we think of the verse in Mark 11:24 that models this, we think, how can we lose? We just pray for what we want, slap God's name at the end of it, and voila! Instant results.

However, this is not what God had in mind as John penned those God-breathed words. God is God. He is not a genie, and He is less interested in granting wishes and requests than He is in refining our character and the lives of those around us. His ways are not our ways, as we are told in Isaiah 55:8. Even the most seemingly godly prayer, like "lead my daughter to salvation right now," may not line up with God's timing. In our desperate efforts to control what we believe should be well within our ability (and even our rights), we sometimes forget that God is in control. It is in Him we "live and move and have our being" (Acts 17:28).

The Bible is filled with people who tried to manipulate God's plans after running out of faith and patience. Sarah had Abraham sleep with her servant girl to father a long-promised child. Jacob's mother Rebekah plotted to trick Isaac into passing on the birthright to Jacob instead of Esau. Both of these actions, and others like them, mock God and defy His original plans and purposes.

And, of course, there are consequences to pay when we take matters like this into our own hands. Both Rebekah and Sarah doubted God's power and felt like they needed to take control of their situations. The result: tribes and descendants who moved further away from God through alternative faith practices and intermarrying into alternative religions.

What we are really doing when we thank God in advance for what He will do is *trusting Him to do it*. We move aside and sit down. We give up our rights to interfere and become the spectators—not the initiators—of plans. We acknowledge that we are children of our Father, God, seeking His will and walking in His ways.

When my older son struggled socially in high school, I prayed for him to blossom and thanked God in advance. High school passed and the results of those prayers were not evident to me—until I took him to college. God was clear in telling me on my son's college campus that fall day that he was exactly where God wanted him and that this was the culmination of all my years of praying. Days later, my son called me to say how happy he was. Since that day, he continues to enjoy a rich social life and is connected to a church. This outcome wasn't reflective of a popularity-filled high school experience I prayed for—it was infinitely better. I'm so grateful God's plans are so much bigger and better than my own.

Keys to Kingdom Living: His ways might not be your ways, but He is working and He is sovereign.

Doorpost: "You may ask me for anything in my name, and I will do it." John 14:14

THANKING GOD—PUBLICLY

*S*ocial media is filled with tips about great malls, online stores, trendy boutiques, and great products to try and buy. It's fun to tell your friends about something you have discovered that has simplified or enriched your life or added to its convenience. And when our spouse or child accomplishes something great, it's an awesome way to express your joy and pride.

But sometimes when blessings come to pass or a promise is fulfilled, we only share it with a smaller group of people. Or maybe, in our busyness or in moving ahead to the next item on our prayer list, we don't acknowledge it to anyone at all. Maybe we only pause for a moment for a quick thanks before moving onto our next hurdle.

I believe that, when we neglect to give God the glory in the telling of His mighty works to one another, we miss an opportunity to glorify Him with fellow believers as well as those yet to step into His marvelous light. There is tremendous power in coming together with others to hear testimonies of how God has worked in our lives. It certainly doesn't mean we should stand on a platform in the middle of the street shouting it through a megaphone. It doesn't even mean we should post it all over Facebook, Twitter, and Instagram. But what it does mean is that we should be bold enough to share it in situations where it's appropriate, natural, and ultimately helpful.

I remember when I was just beginning to attend Bible study. Before getting to know people well, I erroneously assumed no one there had problems as challenging as mine: an adopted child with severe autism, and difficult years ahead filled with intensive care, disappointment, and heartache. Then one day I was sitting on a bench with a woman of few words who would rather clean a thousand toilets than stand up in front of a room and speak. I casually asked her about her children, and she told me about the one in middle school and the other who was in heaven with Jesus. Her story of his short life on earth was not rife with how she was robbed by God or even about the unbearable pain of losing him—though she surely had, and still has, tremendous grief. What she did describe was her hope in Jesus and His plan for her family's life, no matter what it looked like. And though she teared up a bit, I could see that her comments and attitude were genuine. That was a real "Aha!" moment for me. She quietly told me she carries on and trusts in the future because of her relationship with Jesus Christ. Her testimony spoke more volumes to me than a thousand fiery radio sermons ever did.

Don't underestimate the power of your testimony as an overcomer. Be the tenth leper who stops to thank Jesus, not one of the nine who can't be bothered.

Keys to Kingdom Living: Sharing authentically how God works in your life blesses others in tremendous ways and glorifies our Father.

Doorpost: "I will praise You, Lord, with all my heart; I will tell of all the marvelous things You have done." Psalm 9:1

THANKING GOD WITH OUR LIFELONG ACTIONS

*T*he art of thankfulness is slowly being edged out by the rising tide of entitlement. Why should we be thankful, popular culture dictates, when we totally *deserve* the new luxury car, those overpriced shoes, or the break-the-bank engagement ring and wedding? Even the utterance of a "thank you" has eroded as formalities in society ebb with the changing times. I remember my oldest telling me he had a "please and thank you problem" because few of his friends were in the habit of saying it and they were calling him on it.

Of course, as Christians, we are called to remember in James 1:17 that "every good and perfect thing comes from above." It's amazing how counter-cultural this verse really is. Most people curse and blame God when something bad happens, but when they receive a raise or win the lottery, God is not even mentioned as the source of blessing. As Christians, we are called to a life of generosity. We are called to give of our time, our treasures, and even our empathy in entering into the pain of another. If you have ever been on the receiving end of the blessing of having a friend like this, you know what a rare and precious gift results from it. That very friend is from God Himself.

If we are truly in tune with our precious Heavenly Father, we are eager to live a purpose-filled life that reflects the depth of our gratitude to all Jesus Christ has done for us. We recognize that everything we have comes from God, and that we are merely entrusted to manage it all as His stewards. When we recognize and truly accept this responsibility, we can manage our time and talents to maximize this attitude, which in turn can bring great joy to our lives as well.

Because my husband and I have an autistic child, we were unable to stay in hotels with him for years. Once, during a year of great provision, my husband suggested we buy a small vacation home. We decided early on it would also be a place where God's people would meet, and we opened the home for this specific purpose.

Recently, it came time to sell it, and we no longer required many of its furnishings. Although the buyer wanted some of the pieces, others were not needed. At this same time, a young couple just starting out expressed their need for a dining table and chairs. God was clear: give ours to them. (The furniture was installed in their home, and it fits so perfectly, it looks as if it were made for the space.) Next on the list: four extra chairs. Enter an empty youth room at the church, now filled with four places to sit that also look as if they were hand-picked by a decorator. These and other stories of generosity like them point so clearly to God's design for His things—and how we, as the givers, are indeed as blessed as the recipients.

Keys to Kingdom Living: Live a life of generosity with all your resources, sharing burdens and treasures.

Doorpost: "The generous will prosper; those who refresh others will themselves be refreshed." Proverbs 11:25 (NLT)

THANKING GOD IN A SYSTEMATIC
WAY

The tortoise and the hare serve as a lasting testimony to running the sprint and the marathon. In a world of instant gratification, we hop on the treadmill one day and forgo the gym for a Netflix marathon the next. Or save money one month and dip into the kitty thirty days later? Resolve to eliminate sugar, only to dive into some ice cream before the ink is wet on our list of resolutions? We are, after all, human. We are surrounded by the temptation of satisfying our every desire instantaneously.

Adopting a systematic approach to gratitude-filled living is the key to a thankful existence. There are many ways to incorporate thanksgiving into everyday life. When we wake up and are thankful that God has given us another day of this earth, we start out with the right mindset. Morning prayers of thanksgiving during our quiet times also offer a structure for thanksgiving in our lives. The teaching pastor at our church has a daily reminder set to his phone at a time in his day when he says he is most prone to frustration and "thanklessness." By seeing a visual reminder pop up on his phone, he is reminded to take the focus off himself and his wants and put it onto being grateful for the blessings he does have. Technology offers a convenient delivery system to keep him faithful to systematic gratitude during the day. Consistent thankfulness is key to our ability to weather the unexpected problems with grace and an overcoming attitude.

In Daniel 2, King Nebuchadnezzar is terrorized by a dream none of his inner circle of trusted advisors can interpret. Daniel, part of the outer circle, is next up on the proverbial chopping block. Does he freak out with worry and fall into hysterics? No. Instead, he asks his friends to pray for the dream to be revealed. As Daniel sleeps that night, God does just that. Daniel then engages in one of the most beautiful prayers recorded in the Bible. All is well until Daniel is again put to the test when a decree to worship only the king and no other goes into effect. Daniel continues a lifestyle of prayer, even as he knows the penalty for his actions is death. In verse 10 of Daniel 6, we read that Daniel continues his thankful lifestyle: "There, just as he had always done, he knelt down at the open windows and prayed to God three times a day." Daniel was not about to sacrifice his systematic prayer life because of the decree of an earthly king. As you may know from the Bible story of the lion's den, Daniel accepts his fate even as God miraculously intervenes to close the mouths of the lions.

While the results of our systematic prayer may not be this dramatic, prayer honors God, prepares us for when our apple carts topple, and models for the world what it looks like to trust in God no matter what happens. But the key is to "pray without ceasing," as Paul states in 1 Thessalonians 5:16.

Keys to Kingdom Living: Build a continual, structured life of prayer that lines up with God's will for your life.

Doorpost: "Devote yourselves to prayer, being watchful and thankful." Colossians 4:2

THANKING GOD FOR THE SMALL THINGS

*I*n many ways it feels easier to be grateful for the central things in our lives, the big things—our family members, employment, the success of our loved ones. What seems to come less naturally on a daily basis is the thanksgiving for the smaller—but not necessarily less important—blessings we take for granted every day. Do we thank God for the air we breathe, even though without it we would surely expire? Anyone who has been to China, or seen pictures of the polluted air there, does not take clean, breathable air for granted. And anyone who has traveled to Africa and seen the dirty water consumed there doesn't look at a clean glass of water the same ever again.

Yet we are continually sheltered with a blanket of blessings that most of us fail to acknowledge and recognize. Do we thank God for the roof over our heads, or the freedom to worship our chosen religion in public? Are we grateful to God that we can tote our Bibles around, even though in some countries such an act is punishable by death? Are we grateful for an infrastructure of justice and law abidance, however flawed we might perceive it to be? Or do we instead lament how our homes need improvement, how the music in church didn't seem quite up to par, or how we might be too tired to drive to church today? Glass half-full or half-empty? It all depends on your perspective.

Godly perspective on these and other matters of daily blessing helps set the tone for a thankful life. Jesus always blessed the food before He ate with His friends. You never heard Him complaining about His daily bread and the lack of fresh butter or olive oil. He gave His entire life as a "ransom for many," continually sacrificing comfort to achieve His higher purpose. Even on the cross when He was offered vinegar mixed with gall, essentially a painkiller (Mark 15:23), Jesus refused it. His purpose was to pay for the sins of mankind to facilitate redemption.

How often does comfort get in the way of our higher purposes? When we are thankful for the little things, we are blessed with a viewpoint of our lives enriched with blessing, even if we do not view our lives as a reflection of everything we want. I remember hearing a woman who suffered many health problems describe how, every night when she fell into bed, no matter how tired she was, she always remembered to thank God for her warm, dry bed, how comfortable it was, and what a blessing it was every night in her life.

It struck me, as she said that, how I never once expressed my gratitude for my bed. I have tried to make a point of being grateful for a different small thing every day: food in the refrigerator, good health, good friends, and a car that starts in the morning. When problems present themselves, even in these areas, I remind myself of God's blessings. None are a guarantee for happiness. They're part of God's plan for my life, characterized by a blend of abundance and affliction. "Shall we only accept the good things from God?" Job asks rhetorically in Job 2:10. We should do the same.

Keys to Kingdom Living: A lifestyle pleasing to God includes an appreciation of blessings big and small.

Doorpost: "Giving thanks is a sacrifice that truly honors me." Psalm 50:23

THANKING GOD AND MENTORING
OTHERS IN THANKFULNESS

*O*ne of the greatest joys of my active mothering years came on the last Mother's Day before my oldest went away to college. He wrote a greeting on Instagram I will never forget. What especially struck me were these sentences : "She loves and loves and loves! Without her, I don't know what kind of person I would be to others! Thanks, Mom, love you!"

I am humbled to say that, in the raising of my son, God impressed on me to mentor him to be a thankful, loving, and compassionate young man—which he is, by the grace of God. But his key phrase, "I don't know what kind of person I would be to others," serves as a reminder of how important it is to model thankfulness to those younger than us, either in actual years or in their faith journey. A baby might be thrilled when you give her a bottle, but she does not yet have words to express it—thankfulness must be modeled. Even my autistic child, with very few words, was teachable enough that today he can get across the words, "Thank you," and with appropriate cues even sings a short thank-you prayer. Thankfulness does not come naturally; it must be practiced and reinforced through parents, friends, and through the reading of God's Word.

We can mentor others in three important ways: We can express our gratitude for all we have to be thankful for in our own lives. We can allow others to see our actions of gratitude through service to others. And we can help others discover and celebrate the things in their own lives they have to be thankful for. Then they, in turn, can share them, be a blessing to others, and eventually mentor the next generation themselves.

There are many practical ways to encourage this. Keeping a gratitude journal is one way to remind ourselves (and those we are mentoring) how much we have to be thankful for. Taking "mentees" to a homeless shelter to see people less fortunate than themselves is another way to help illuminate the gratitude "chamber" in our minds by reminding us of blessings we take for granted. My son was forever changed after handing out Christmas presents to orphans and building houses for under-served Mexican nationals. And encouraging your mentee to identify someone younger than they with whom to share these lessons is yet another step in sharing the wisdom and knowledge you've acquired.

There is no better antidote to the materialism of our consumer culture than practicing gratitude.

Keys to Kingdom Living: Model and mentor gratitude to those young in years or young in their spiritual walk.

Doorpost: "Repeat [God's commands] again and again to your children. . . . Write them on the doorposts of your house and on your gates." Deuteronomy 6:7, 9 (NLT)

WEEK 3: DISTANCE FROM GOD

DISTANCE FROM GOD: BETWEEN
HEAD AND HEAD

*Y*ou've probably heard before that the distance between your mind and your heart is infinitely longer than the twelve inches or so that it measures. Our mind knows not to reach for that chocolate bar, but our heart aches with longing and leaves the mind's reasoning in the dust. But when it comes to matters of God, this distance can be disastrous. The God-shaped hole in everyone's heart is not always sensibly cared for by the mind, and sometimes our mind even creates a barrier.

There is a reason why, in Colossians 3:2, we read to "set our minds on things above, not on earthly things." Self-help books (and even some misguided theologians!) are filled with suggestions that everything we need to achieve divine peace is within us. When we trust in our own decision-making or let our feelings and thoughts wander, we are not inclined to drift to God. We can't expect our boats to float to their destinations; we must follow a map. Or, one step farther, we must follow the course of the map's cartographer. We didn't make the map—we aren't the cartographers, we are the travelers!

Fortunately, our cartographer Jesus Christ has laid out each journey for those whose names are written in His glorious Book of Life. Though no two journeys will look alike, He does supply tools and blueprints for how we can all build and prepare our inner temples to fully receive Him. As we "set our minds" on things above, we immerse ourselves in His Word, surround ourselves with His people and reduce our focus on things of this world. You've probably heard the saying that, if you feel far away from God, guess who moved? The antidote for feeling distanced from God is to modify your schedule to maximize your time, exposure, and even your goals to reflect your love and devotion. Just saying you believe in God does not make you a Christ follower. One look at a person's calendar can tell a casual observer what is important to that person in an instant.

Next, we remind ourselves of our divine objective: seeking God unceasingly. Proverbs 8:17 says, "A heart who seeks God finds Him." You might read this and think of a friend or relative who seems to be seeking something that continues to elude them.

We all have a hole inside us that we try to fill with a variety of things. In reality, God designed us with a soul designed to be filled with His love. Those who don't have a relationship with Jesus tend to fill this hole with everything but the One True God. But we don't casually gravitate toward holiness any more than we are inclined to stumble onto God. The path to seeking God requires direction. Such a desire must be properly guided, perhaps by another Christian, and certainly by the Holy Spirit's divine intervention. This is precisely why we need to keep all seekers continually on our radar, so we can help guide them in their life journeys, always pointing to the One who gave us our hope and even asking God to continually renew, redirect, and prevent the heart-to-mind distance from wreaking havoc in our spiritual journeys.

Keys to Kingdom Living: Keep your mind and heart God-focused as you cling to Him and give glory to God in your devotion and by example to others.

Doorpost: "And the peace of God, which surpasses all understanding, will guard your hearts and your minds in Christ Jesus." Philippians 4:7 (ESV)

DISTANCE FROM GOD: YOU AND YOUR BIBLE

*E*arly on, when I began my closer walk with Jesus, I was sitting with a group of mature Christians at Bible study. One who had been following Jesus for more than fifty years said something I will never forget: "Isn't it embarrassing when you get a new Bible, and it's not dog-eared or full of written notes?" The comment took my breath away. Mine might as well have had the plastic seal still around it! I chuckled to myself and hoped no one would examine my pristine book too closely.

Today, dog-eared pages and notes are part of my book's fabric. I will say that I would not be the same Christ follower today were it not for the tremendous benefits of a systematic Bible study group filled with godly mentors and young women hungry for example and direction. Whether your Bible is an app on your phone, available in fifty translations on your iPad, or the print version you lug around, as long as you are *in the Word*, and *doing the Word*, it does not matter. Even if you've just cracked open the plastic seal on your Bible, that's okay, too. Move forward in faith and determination.

Being in constant communion with God's Word ensures several things. Aside from the obvious—that God commands it —continually bathing yourself in God's Word reminds us of His infinite love and promises and gives us the hope we need. It is, in fact, "perfect, reviving the soul; the testimony of the Lord is sure

. . . [His words are] more to be desired than gold . . . Sweeter also than honey" (Psalm 19). So sweet is God's Word to the believer that Ezekiel himself ingested it in the third chapter of his book, declaring it as sweet as honey.

How do we ingest God's Word? Are we clinging to every word, pondering its sweetness as a compass for our lives? Or are we making out a mental to-do list when the Word is read aloud in church? Or do we even try to question or amend God's Word, leaving out His laws so we can lead compartmentalized lives? When we remain in God's Word, we crowd out flawed and deceptive cultural wisdom.

Naturally, hearing the Word isn't enough. Jesus had plenty to say about hearing and doing of the Word. In James 1:23–25 He says, "Anyone who listens to the Word but does not do what it says is like someone who looks at his face in the mirror and, after looking at himself, goes away and immediately forgets what he looks like. But whoever looks intently into the perfect law that gives freedom, and continues in it . . . will be blessed in what they do." What a beautiful promise!

Keys to Kingdom Living: We remain in the palm of God's hand when we immerse ourselves in His precious Word, continually reminding us of His love and promises.

Doorpost: "Everyone then who hears these words of mine and does them will be like a wise man who built his house on the rock." Matthew 7:24 (ESV)

DISTANCE FROM GOD: YOUR TIME WITH, OR WITHOUT, HIM

*Y*ou're to be commended that you're reading this now, because you have already taken the first step today in spending time with God. The fact that you have carved out this time means you recognize the importance of hearing from God in your day.

Daily benefits of a quiet time are as numerous as they are life changing. Perhaps the most crucial aspect of this time is that it provides the intimacy required for close relationship. We need a dialogue with God available through our petitions—and even silence—as we carve out a space for God to speak. Even Jesus made sure He withdrew from His large crowd of followers to spend time alone with His Father, as is recounted numerous times in the New Testament.

Because relationship with God is on an unseen level, we must be more deliberate in the carving out of time with Him. We do not literally see Him standing before us, yet He is always there and available to us when we feel lonely, sad, confused, or even grateful for something wonderful happening in our lives. God is our father, provider, protector, savior, giver of life, advisor, righteous judge, and the best friend we will ever have. Unlike others in our lives, He does not demand, but He does seek us. "Behold, I stand at the door and knock. If anyone hears my voice and opens the door, I will come in to him," He says in Revelation 3:20.

The debate about the times, places, conditions, and parameters of quiet time are widely debated in Christian circles. Many believe this time should be first thing in the morning, so that each precious day is properly framed by God. While it's certainly true that this is the ideal, sometimes people fall into the trap of thinking that, if they have not done their quiet time first thing in the morning, they missed the boat and should start over tomorrow. Any time with God each day is better than none. If your baby woke you up at four a.m., spending quiet time in the late morning is pleasing to God. He knows your heart—and a heart that seeks God finds Him (Jeremiah 29:13). Some days you may linger at your desk and sing or listen to praise music, light a candle, or journal. Other days you may lock yourself in a bathroom or closet for the privacy you need to fall on your knees to ask for guidance for an impossible day ahead, or plead for help and mercy after an especially hard day.

Being with God also reminds us of God's laws as we face a temptation-riddled day. We are more inclined to do the right thing when we have just been reminded of exactly what it was. We will be more loving to our family and friends, a better neighbor, a more considerate driver, and compassionate citizen as we face continual opportunities to give and sacrifice like Jesus did when we are reminded of His flawless example.

Keys to Kingdom Living: Daily time with God is an investment well spent.

Doorpost: "The Lord is near to all who call on Him . . . He hears their cry and saves them. The Lord watches over all who love Him." Psalm 145:18–20

DISTANCE FROM GOD: BELIEF VERSUS COMMITMENT

$\mathcal{W}$e can ingest God's Word, believe what it says, and even occasionally follow through in the doing of the Word—but if our goals, actions, and life objectives do not match up with them, we aren't living the full life God means for us to live.

A man I know has spent countless hours poring over God's Word, church history, and countless liturgical volumes in his quest for knowledge. He is the kind of no-nonsense intellectual whose life mirrored more of a high achiever and scholar than servant. After years of amassing book knowledge, he began to enter into service to others. Early on, he shared with me that, as he was engaging with a developmentally disabled young man, he saw what he believed to be the face of Jesus superimposed onto this man's face. This relayed experience framed his view of service moving forward, because he had experienced a powerful reminder of Whom we are serving.

Though we call ourselves followers of the Most High God, how closely do our beliefs and actions align? Do we go out of our way to help the homeless man in front of the store, or out of our way so we don't run into him (like the self-righteous religious leaders in the parable of the Good Samaritan who could not be bothered)? The Bible is filled with people who thought they knew better than God did. Take Jonah, for example. When

Jonah boarded a boat rather than go to Nineveh as God had commanded, God put Jonah in a very stinky three-day, three-night time-out in the belly of a large fish until he came to his senses and was ready to follow God's command. God did what He needed to do in order to get his attention, and He continues this practice today.

A few months back, my oldest son and I were leaving church in the midst of scorching temperatures. We had a heavy agenda: meeting friends for his going-away lunch, picking up a few things he needed for college, then hosting a going-away dinner that night in our home. As we climbed into the car, a woman I knew from church asked if she could have a ride. Though every fiber in my being fought to say no, I said yes, and she climbed into the car. Once we dropped her off, my son, slightly irritated, asked me why I agreed to do it when we were clearly going to be thrown off schedule. I simply said that in life we don't always do what we feel like doing; instead, we do what is right. I almost missed this teachable moment by giving into my fleshly inclination.

Keys for Kingdom Living: Serving others demonstrates an understanding of—and commitment to—God's laws.

Doorpost: "I was hungry, and you fed me. I was thirsty, and you gave me a drink. I was a stranger, and you invited me in your home. I was naked, and you gave me clothing. I was sick, and you cared for me. I was in prison, and you visited me."
Matthew 25:35-36

DISTANCE FROM GOD: SIN NOT CONFESSED

*O*ne aspect of our weekly Sabbath meetings with God which is de-emphasized in Christian culture today is the act of confession. Some churches believe this act should be private and requires more time than church will allow. Others believe that anyone visiting church who is still trapped in their shame will find the nature of this practice uncomfortable and off-putting.

Building this practice into our quiet time is one way to make sure we "take out the garbage," so to speak, and move on to our renewed commitment to God. But when we let our wrongdoings fester, or even possibly put them out of our minds entirely, we deny ourselves the deepest communion possible with God.

Once, when my oldest son was about five years old, he did something to anger me. I was furious with him and told him to go to his room and think about what he had done wrong. I needed a time-out from him, as well. An hour later he came downstairs crying, saying, "I need love." For him, at that time, the breach in relationship was more than he could bear. He apologized and we mended fences. His apology did not undo what he'd done wrong, but he genuinely expressed regret—and I needed to forgive him, just as Christ forgives us when we come to Him with a contrite heart.

Breaks in our relationship with God, and the resulting

distance, are sometimes less obvious to us, especially at first. The white lie we tell to worm out of a meeting turns into a web of deceit. The flirtatious comment at work turns into a secret rendezvous, leading to initially unforeseen paths of destruction for everyone concerned.

Maybe we miss church one Sunday for a trip, then the next Sunday it's less of a big deal to miss again, and before you know it, over time you haven't been in a month. But each of those missed Sabbaths represents a break with one of God's commandments. As human beings, we rationalize. We compartmentalize. We tell ourselves that law is really for *other* people. We are told in Psalm 1:2 to "meditate on the law day and night," so our delight will be in the Lord and His precepts.

Personal acts of confession should be regular and all-inclusive. We should not only confess those things while they are fresh in our minds, we should ask God to bring to mind any sin either unknown to us or forgotten by us—our memories and consciences are far from infallible. By confessing before God, we embrace the sacrifice of Jesus Christ and all the power it carries in our lives to move forward in obedience, faith, and service to Him.

Keys to Kingdom Living: Don't let sin create a barrier between you and God.

Doorpost: "Whoever conceals their sins does not prosper, but the one who confesses and renounces them finds mercy." Proverbs 28:13

DISTANCE FROM GOD: COMPARTMENTALIZED BREAKS WITH GOD'S LAW

A more serious—and sometimes harder to rectify—break from God occurs when we engage in a systematic pattern of willful disobedience to God. Without exception, any break with God's law is grieved by Him. But we dig an even deeper pit when we commit the same sin over and over again, perhaps by misinterpreting God's law or bending its truth to suit our own desires. We water down God's law and its weight in our own lives when we do not follow it to the letter.

When an unmarried couple decides to engage in sexual relations outside of God's law, they might rationalize it by telling themselves they plan to marry soon. Someone regularly stealing money from their company might tell himself he is owed the money because he has been unfairly paid for years. These kinds of sins begin to establish a pattern in the lives of those who commit them, taking them down a slippery slope where they begin to view their own judgment as superior to God's.

When we see ourselves like God and try to dilute His laws, we create a gulf so large and seemingly impossible to bridge that only Jesus Christ can remove it. But often pride rears its ugly head. It leads us into the trap and sometimes prevents us from getting out of it. Like Eve who, as recorded in Genesis, bit into the fruit in an attempt to achieve godly wisdom, we fall into the trap of thinking sometimes we know better than God (even if we don't actually come right out and say it). Our actions tell the sad tale for themselves.

The best way to avoid this kind of systematic sin is to remain rooted in the Word so we can recognize a breach from God's law before it becomes a routine part of our life choices. The tenth time we take God's name in vain, what we say rolls off of our tongue much easier than it did the first time. When Peter denied Jesus three times on the night before He was crucified, it wasn't until the rooster crowed for the third time, as Jesus predicted, that Peter realized the weight of what he had done in denying he even knew Jesus. We read in Luke 22:61 that Jesus "turned and looked straight at Peter."

Though we are not face-to-face with Jesus in the same way Peter was, He is always watching us. We read in 2 Chronicles 16:9: "The eyes of the Lord run to and fro throughout the earth . . ." The next time we are tempted to do something that we know deep down is wrong, whether it is for the first time or the hundredth, we would do well to imagine Jesus looking us straight in the eye. He sees our every move and knows our every thought. Thankfully, He is also there to forgive if we humble ourselves and ask forgiveness, acknowledging that He is God and we are not!

Keys to Kingdom Living: When we dilute God's law, we make ourselves gods and set ourselves up for spiritual failure.

Doorpost: "If we say we have no sin, we deceive ourselves, and the truth is not in us." 1 John 1:8

DISTANCE FROM GOD:
ACCOUNTABILITY TO OURSELVES
FIRST AND OTHERS SECOND

*W*hen it comes to telling others what they should be doing, as opposed to what we ourselves are doing, we should only be as obedient to our own best advice.

As a mother, I have found that my standards for my children are often far higher than the ones I set for myself. It's embarrassing how much easier it is to find the holes in the Swiss cheese of your child's life choices than it is to find them in your own life. I remember telling my oldest son to forgive one of his friends for what he did to him, when he quickly pointed out to me that I had yet to forgive the child's mother for something she did to me long ago: busted!

I have found my children to be expert pin-pointers of my pride and my desire to instruct. My autistic son in particular, who is nonverbal for the most part, had apparently had enough of my corrections. One afternoon when he was really trying to please me by doing everything I'd asked, he looked me straight in the eyes and said, "Good boy." Right then it hit me, the truth from Ephesians 6:4: "do not exasperate your children, instead bring them up in the training and instruction of the Lord." Training involves modeling, and all good leaders, secular and Christian, know that anyone who is being trained learns best by example. If we want our kids to tell the truth, we can't tell our friend on the phone that we are still at the store when we are home standing in the kitchen. We can't tell our kids not to take candy bars from the store if they see us sampling from the bulk candy bin in the produce department.

Jesus talks about the conditions required for correcting others. In Matthew 7:3, He points out that it's best to take out the plank in your own eye before you remove the speck of sawdust from someone else's. In other words, whatever is wrong in your own life is a much bigger priority than helping someone else with their problem. After all, if everyone were judicious at removing their own planks, there would be no sawdust to concern ourselves with. Pride often is the improper motivator in correction of others: we have it all together and they don't.

Thankfully, not all interventions are self-righteous in nature. Correction from friends done with the right heart motivation can lead to repentance and restored relationship with God. You may have been on the receiving or giving end of such an interaction, with positive results. When Nathan told David a parable in 2 Samuel 12 illustrating the very thing David had done wrong (without mentioning any names), David initially failed to recognize that he was the sinner in the story. David, as acting king, said, "As the Lord lives, the man who has done this will surely die." When Nathan plainly told David he was the man Nathan meant, he immediately repented.

Keys to Kingdom Living: When we are close to God, committed to obedience and habitual confession, we are positioned to help others with any sawdust issues that may arise in their lives.

Doorpost: "Let your light shine before others, that they may see your good deeds and glorify your Father in heaven." Matthew 5:16

WEEK 4: CULTURAL CAMOUFLAGE

CULTURAL CAMOUFLAGE: GOD'S PEOPLE JUST SAY NO

*I*nbred in our human nature is a deep desire to be loved and accepted by everyone. For some people, this people-pleasing desire becomes a stronghold and sometimes even an obstacle in their daily living. I struggle with this issue myself, so I have to guard against blending into society as a Christ follower who wants to make a difference.

Even before Jesus appeared in this world, men such as Noah and John the Baptist were not exactly icons of the "in crowd." Noah worked on the ark for what is estimated by theologians to be fifty-five to seventy-five years, no doubt enduring barbs from incredulous neighbors reacting with great skepticism to his flood talk. John the Baptist probably looked more like a homeless man than the great prophet and diviner of God's plans and purposes, munching on locusts, honey dripping from his beard, all the while traipsing around in a musky camel hair toga. Though not exactly "A-listers" in their community, these men exhibited such great courage and faultless obedience that they changed the course of human history. In fact, it is interesting to note that while John the Baptist grew in popularity, it was his message and not his image that attracted people to him to such a degree that he was mistaken for the Messiah by some zealous followers.

Are people attracted to your "message"? Are you coura-geous in your Christian life? Or do you blend into the background, looking like everyone else around you? Do you stand up for God's agenda or adopt the ideals of whoever is standing in front of you to keep the peace? I'm not advocating standing up on a box in the town square and foisting ideas on people you don't know. That isn't the best approach to attract people to God. I'm talking about sharing with people with whom you're emotionally invested. Do you share with them the hope you have and need?

I remember sitting in church next to our translator in Rwanda with my mission team on the last day of our ten-day mission trip. As I waited for my turn to speak, he turned to me and gave me one of the nicest compliments of my life. He said, "It feels good to be around you—you give out God's love." I wish I could tell you that was always the case, but I am quite human after all. Even so, his comment served as a reminder of what kind of an effect and impact that we can have on others, especially when we share with them the source of our hope and joy. We need to set aside the standard issue camouflage of this world. We need to nip bad language in the bud, skip the inappropriate music mix or obscene TV show, and resist the urge for hand gestures at the inconsiderate driver. When we exercise that kind of self-control, people take notice and sometimes even change their own behavior, even if it is only out of deference to you. Whatever the reason, you have helped someone come up higher.

Keys to Kingdom Living: Forgo quests for popularity and stand out as a Christ follower, no matter what it costs you.

Doorpost: "Do not conform to the pattern of this world . . ." Romans 12:2

CULTURAL CAMOUFLAGE: HOW
EASILY BLENDING OCCURS

Anyone who has ever been to a sports stadium knows that wearing team colors is a huge bonding activity for fans. It's not uncommon for fans to don the sportswear and even paint their faces. Often stadiums are visibly divided according to these colors, perhaps with an occasional dissenter.

Have you ever tried to locate someone in a large crowd where everyone is wearing the same color? It's nearly impossible. When everything looks the same, it's harder for the eye to distinguish minute differences. On cruise ships, travelers are told to bring a distinguishing ribbon to help differentiate their luggage inside holding rooms where all the bags are stored. You may have worn like colors or ordered special shirts for wear at theme parks in an effort to keep your group together.

In the world, where God's agenda takes a back seat to the "if it feels good, do it" mantra, political correctness and popular opinion set the stage for a sameness that should be difficult for a Christ-follower to swallow. Meth addicts, occult practitioners, gang members, and corrupt politicians are glorified and humanized with frightening results. The creators of movies and TV shows that portray these things often recreate a kind of Robin Hood reality within the framework of the show. They suggest that, say, because the protagonist is terminally ill, there is a small gray area where a case could be made for how he must provide for the future for his family. This kind of thinking is as dangerous individually as it is collectively. As Christians we are told in Colossians 3:2 to "set our minds on things above, not on earthly things."

Balance is required to live in the world but not be "of it." We've seen the "NOTW" (Not Of This World) bumper stickers. But we can't set ourselves so apart from the world that we are unable to penetrate and rescue the lost. That's why we're here! We should plainly stand up for God's agenda and truths when asked but do so with "gentleness and respect," as we read in 1 Peter 3:15. We can "stand" without "grandstanding." There is nothing gentle or respectful about bombing clinics in the name of Jesus.

We influence people with our devotion to God through self–sacrifice. Mother Teresa gave up a life of privilege to serve the poorest of the poor for her entire adult life. Corrie ten Boom saved the lives of an estimated 800 Dutch Jews only to be sent to concentration camp. Both sacrificed their lives.

Keys to Kingdom Living: Authentic modeling of the Christian life involves distinguishing yourself from corrupt culture.

Doorpost: "Follow God's example . . . as dearly loved children." Ephesians 5:1

CULTURAL CAMOUFLAGE: STANDING UP VERSUS LYING DOWN

*T*wo kinds of people make up our "in-your-face" culture: the confrontational and the non-confrontational. Confrontational types blare their views. Some become angered when others don't share their opinions. Non-confrontational types are more inclined to avoid debate or change an offending subject to keep the peace and their desired level of harmony. Even in non-denominational Christian settings, dividing issues can rear their troublesome heads. It's important for the Christian to know when to engage and when agreeing to disagree can be a good kind of diffusing camo.

As part of my tenure in leadership at an interdenominational Bible study, we are taught extensively on how to discern between important issues and less crucial topics that may divide the group. Our primary purpose is to attract people to godly living, through example and by the study of His Word.

These so-called "salvation issues" include salvation through grace as opposed to earning your way to heaven. The literal resurrection from the dead by Jesus Christ is another. Admitting flawed natures, confessing sins and inviting Jesus into our heart are all crucial action steps to salvation by anyone of the age and mindset capable of doing so. Of course, clinging to salvation itself is also key. We are called to stand firm in our faith, no matter what the cost, and Christians who are martyred for their faith make the ultimate stand for God, often enduring horrific deaths.

Some issues require more tolerance, such as observing the Sabbath on Saturday instead of Sunday, whether or not to celebrate Halloween, whether or not makeup or tattoos should be worn, which movies, songs or TV programs should be viewed, and whether it is acceptable to drink certain beverages. Godly people who subscribe to views alternative to our own deserve respect; God's Word tells us that if they believe in the Lord Jesus Christ, they will be saved. Our only concern for them, as well as for those who are lost, is that salvation. We must work together on the common ground we share as kingdom builders.

We should offer up "arrow" prayers in situations when we're unsure what God is calling us to say. Jesus often said nothing when He could have launched into great debates about God's sovereignty. When you're with people who enjoy arguing for sheer sport, you would do well not to "give what is holy to the dogs; or cast your pearls before swine," as we are told in Matthew 7:6. Paul warns against our propensity to park our duffs on the judgment throne where they do not belong. "For why is my freedom being judged by another's conscience?" he asks in 1 Corinthians 10:29.

Keys to Kingdom Living: Work to stress common, rather than dissenting, ground among believers.

Doorpost: "[Be] diligent to preserve the unity of the Spirit in the bond of peace." Ephesians 4:3 (NASB)

CULTURAL CAMOUFLAGE: HOW AND
WHEN IT'S GOD-PLEASING TO BLEND
INTO SOCIETY

*O*ne of the most controversial agenda items Jesus undertook was socializing with "marginalized" individuals. His very own reputation as a godly man was continually called into question because of this. His encounters with tax collectors like Zacchaeus, women of lower reputation like the Canaanite, the mentally ill, the demonically possessed, and the lower societal rung of children shaped the opinions of others and even became fodder for gossip among those who sought to dismantle Jesus's followers.

Undoubtedly the most pointed remark regarding this criticism can be paraphrased from Matthew 9:12: "Healthy people don't need a doctor—sick people do." Jesus was less interested in hobnobbing in the temple with the great Hebrew scholars of the day than He was in trying to reach and save the lost. He made that clear in His parable of the shepherd who leaves his ninety-nine sheep to find the one that was lost, and who rejoices more over the recovered animal than he did over the ninety-nine who did not get away. Likewise, Jesus's tale of the prodigal son further illustrates His love for those who have yet to discover the only way to truly fill the God-shaped hole in their hearts.

Do we share His zeal for the lost sheep? Or do we, like the Levite, when faced with the opportunity to help the man in the road left for dead, prefer to pass on the other side without getting our hands dirty? We can probably think of instances when we have been in both camps. However, because we are charged with the responsibility of "making disciples" as the Great Commission states at the end of Matthew, we need to view how we carefully move forward.

The apostle Paul had an awesome approach to winning souls. He said in 1 Corinthians 9:19 that he "made himself a servant to all, that I might win more [souls]. To the Jews, I became as a Jew, in order to win Jews." This does not mean that Paul denounced his faith in Jesus Christ. It means he was willing to socialize with them and blend in with them in order to gain favor and eventually a foothold to share the good news with them.

For example, when godly women take personal grooming items to a strip club and establish relationships with the women who work there, they aren't taking their clothes off—they are ministering to the marginalized as Jesus did. When church members serve breakfast to drug-addicted homeless men living in rundown motels, they aren't taking drugs with them—they are providing food and drink "to the least of these" and, in turn, serving Jesus Christ. We can't influence until we infiltrate.

Keys to Kingdom Living: Seek out ways to infiltrate marginalized areas of society to bring your salt and light as Jesus did, without compromising yourself in the process.

Doorpost: "I have become all things to all people so that by all possible means I might save some. I do all this for the sake of the gospel, that I may share in its blessings." 1 Corinthians 9:22–23

CULTURAL CAMOUFLAGE: USING YOUR FILTER

*N*owhere are my senses more bombarded than when I am in Las Vegas. I remember walking down the strip as the temperature shot to 106 degrees. I was dripping with sweat and my mouth was parched. Suddenly a voice bellowed from a loudspeaker: "You're hot, you're tired, and you're *really* thirsty." The creepy experience was only heightened by the fact that everything in that statement was true. Hearing an unidentifiable voice lay out my vulnerability gave me great pause: the truth hurt! I didn't need an audible reminder! I was just trying to get back to my cold hotel room without stopping yet again at the M&M store or peeking inside one more pricey boutique to buy something I didn't need.

Of course in Vegas the main objective of the city is to not only meet your needs but your desires—not all of which should be met. Our sinful nature is capable of running amok in far less tempting venues, but Vegas does seem to bring out what one hotel advertiser refers to as "the right amount of wrong." Images of perverted sexuality, gluttony, and avarice are everywhere. God is, of course, grieved by all wrongdoing. That's why, wherever we are, we need to make sure our filters are working properly. If we're in church and someone is gossiping, our filter needs to catch the refuse before it takes root. In channel surfing, when inappropriate images are thrust before us, we keep moving or even order Clear Channel so they don't come up at all.

Our filters need to be employed long before our conscience is pricked. The best way to ensure this will happen is to continue to study and devote ourselves to God's Word. If we don't familiarize ourselves with the truth, how can we expect to recognize a lie or prevent a misstep in our walk with God? This requires filtering out words and images not pleasing to God. I read about a pastor who was seated on an airplane next to a guy looking at pornographic images on a computer. He prayed that his seatmate would close his device so that he would not be tempted further. In the meantime, he averted his glance and employed his filter.

If a kid is in a candy store and wants a chocolate bar but is short a few cents, he might think about slipping the chocolate into his pocket. If he is a Christian, he might picture the words "thou shalt not steal." If his filter is working properly, he will refrain from stealing, put the bar back on the shelf, and leave the store.

In this broken world, our filters occasionally fail. Burk Parsons tweeted this little jewel back in January of 2015: "You can tell your faith is real if when the Holy Spirit pricks your conscience, you bleed repentance." Thankfully, we don't have to sit in our shame: Jesus Christ provided a bridge to forgiveness to all who genuinely seek it.

Keys to Kingdom Living: Filtering out ungodly images and ideas keeps us from dishonoring God.

Doorpost: "But as for you . . . flee [all kinds of evil]. Pursue righteousness, godliness, faith, love, steadfastness, gentleness." 1 Timothy 6:11 (ESV)

CULTURAL CAMOUFLAGE: PUTTING ON THE ARMOR

*T*hough a filter is required to navigate images and words, it's no match for Satan himself. We need to make sure our high-caliber filter is paired with the armor of God for optimal protection. If we are called on to explain our intolerance for a matter which is spelled out clearly in the Bible but not commonly accepted in today's "tolerant" society, we need to make sure we are protected to battle.

Satan would love nothing more than to undermine your points to anyone seeking truth, whether truth is delivered by you or sought after from another source. But he is also keen on toppling your convictions in the process. Just as we would not engage in combat or play a sport without protective equipment, we are not to blindly step into cultural conflict without our armor.

What exactly is the armor of God? It is God's protection for our whole lives: we are outfitted at the waist with truth. He gives us a breastplate of His righteousness and footwear adorned with the gospel of peace. We have a shield of faith to protect us from Satan's arrows and the helmet of salvation to protect our mind. Finally, God outfits us with the sword of the Spirit, which is the precious Word of God.

Doug Batchelor, in his article "The Armor of God," lays out the high-stakes faceoff with Satan in this manner: "The battleground for this intense spiritual struggle is not some piece of earthly real estate; it is the human heart." Our very souls are at stake. And without the armor of God, we don't stand a chance. Satan has a wide open target without any real defense mechanism in place. Determination and willpower cannot hold a candle either to God-power or that of Satan, who is a wily adversary and a force with which to be reckoned. We are told in James 4:7 to submit ourselves to God, so that we may resist the Devil and flee from him.

True protection involves using God's armor intentionally and consistently. Both require discipline and consistency. To be protected one day by praying for the armor of the God, and not another because we forget to ask, is to leave ourselves vulnerable. If only our bodies would emit a reminding buzzer when we forget, like our cars do when we forget to buckle our seat belts. Sadly, when we forget to put on the armor of God, we might only be reminded of our neglect when we view the damage done. Getting alone with God to meditate on His Word, acknowledging His sovereignty and our dependency, thanking Him for His blessings, and petitioning Him for help and guidance—all these lay the groundwork for battle dressing.

Keys for Kingdom Living: Seeking the protection of God's armor intentionally and consistently is the best defense against sin and temptation.

Doorpost: "Put on the whole armor of God, that you may be able to stand against the schemes of the devil." Ephesians 6:11 (ESV)

CULTURAL CAMOUFLAGE: HELPING OTHERS WITH THEIR ARMOR AND FILTERS

*J*ust as we rely on mature Christians to guide us in truth and godly living, so we are called to mentor others in these important practices. Part of this duty involves knowing what is right and doing it. We are given a solid example in James 1:24 of a person who listens to the Word but does not do it. He is like a man who sees himself in the mirror and then forgets what he looks like. Our reflection to ourselves, and to others as well, should be that of a mirror image to Jesus Christ. In mirroring Him, we share with others how to submit to God, acknowledging that He puts His armor on us, and showing them how to use their filters, just as we do.

When I began working with youth, I remember being surprised at the number of steps involved before our church permitted someone to actually begin their tasks and responsibilities. Fingerprinting by the FBI, pages of questions about personal habits, and even behavior covenants to sign. But these steps were more than just hoops to jump through; they were checkpoints to keep negative influences away from impressionable youth. Students are studying more than just academics as they mature. They are watching the adults in their lives to make sure their walk lines up with their talk, especially when those adults are entrusted with their spiritual well-being. We can't tell kids to put on the sword of truth and then lie in front of them about a matter we deem unimportant. When we tell them to put on the helmet of salvation, we need to make sure we aren't watching inappropriate images in a movie that we can never "un-see."

Modeling the processes of filtering and dressing for daily battles with temptation is important, but arming a young person with helpful books and verses is another way to ready them for their ever-challenging world. Be authentic in your sharing and enter into their world. We are told in Galatians 6:2 to "carry each other's burdens, and in this way you will fulfill the law of Christ." We need to be honest and forthcoming about what it means to struggle and really try to understand what young people go through in the fast-changing world in which we all live. By acknowledging the existence and levity of the struggle, and reminding them of the tools available to them as Christ followers, we truly carry their burdens and can pray alongside them for encouragement to help them go the distance.

I remember the first time my oldest son became annoyed when a fire truck and accident scene delayed us from arriving at a destination on time. God gave me wisdom in the moment and I said to him, "Instead of being upset, let's pray for everyone involved that no one was seriously hurt, and if they have not committed to Jesus, that this is their go-to moment." As he got older, he ended up reminding *me*. Today he and I individually commit to praying this prayer whenever possible.

Keys for Kingdom Living: Model and instruct new Christians in arming themselves for battle and using their filters to keep them on a godly path.

Doorpost: "Train a child up in the way he should go; even when he is old he will not depart from it." Proverbs 22:6 (ESV)

WEEK 5: TESTING 1, 2, 3

TESTING 1, 2, 3: SHOWING YOUR WORK

*W*hen I was in college, I was asked to tutor my boss's son who worked at our local polo club where I was a door hostess. I remember being struck by how dramatically school procedures had changed, with an ever-increasing accountability for each step of the student's work. Teachers today often insist on seeing the rough drafts for every paper. Cheating had become rampant, just as it is today. Showing computations and rough drafts also reinforces the notion that the work along the way is just as important as the finished product.

So when it comes to working and growing in our spiritual life, we can fool ourselves with deceitful schemes, but "God is not mocked," as we read in Galatians 6:7. In our journey of life, Jesus Christ is actually more interested in what you will do with your life leading up to the day you die. He will be re-examining your scratch paper from His judgment seat when He comes again in glory. The scratch paper where you "show your work" is where the rubber really meets the road. Any one of us can spout out Bible verses and give elaborate speeches on the right way to live, but if our scratch paper does not resemble the final draft others see and hear about, we have not passed God's test of faithfulness. The trusting flock of believers who later found out their married pastor's name was listed on a hook-up website were shocked to learn their leader's scratch paper did not match up with his Sunday morning messages. Sadly, this resulted in disaster for them, the man's family, and for the man himself.

Not all missteps are as public as that particular pastor's, but they all grieve God and require atonement before Him. I know my own scratch paper is rife with cross outs, do-overs, and other starts and stops. We don't want the world to view our mistake-ridden scrap, preferring the final draft on pristine parchment that will hopefully reflect a life as wholly dedicated to God as is humanly possible in our imperfect world.

Thankfully, when we do mess up, we don't need to sit in our shame and take up residence with regret. When we genuinely repent of our sins, Jesus is right there with His eraser, wiping clean the slate for us to begin again as a new creation. And if we live an authentic life, we don't hide our mistakes and the scratch paper from others—or even from ourselves. Our missteps can serve as a blueprint for keeping our feet on the straight and narrow path God sets before us. We can be transparent with others in relaying how we are redeemed and preserved by God's grace, and often others can learn from our mistakes. Scratch paper with those kinds of notes is worth mining for the gold it contains for pursuing God with our whole hearts.

Keys for Kingdom Living: Review your scratch paper and show your work to others to help yourself and others come up higher.

Doorpost: "But He knows the way that I take; when He has tested me, I will come forth as gold." Job 23:10

TESTING 1, 2, 3: THE DANGER OF SHORTCUTS

J grew up in a house with a mother who was a perfectionist about everything she undertook. The word "shortcut" was never a part of her approach to anything. Procedure was paramount for achieving the highest and best result. My mom was the kind of exacting homemaker who would hover over a stove all day to prepare homemade court bouillon to use in making her coq au vin. She did not trust the food processor to chop her parsley fine enough for her escargot bourguignon, preferring instead to repeatedly wield her exquisitely sharp knife over the unruly sprigs to achieve her ultimate desired result.

I did not initially inherit my mother's love for perfection. I was fascinated by the idea of the shortcut. Ways home no one knew about. Substituting ingredients without having to go to the store. My fascination with alternative approaches naturally led to some disasters. For instance, substituting cilantro for parsley does not ensure a tasty soup, but instead results in a culinary disaster that involved a four-hour evacuation of our tiny newlywed nest. Do not try this at home!

When it comes to following God's directions, our notion of a shortcut always fails to line up with God's plan. Not only that, the origin of a shortcut that runs counter to God's plan is always from Satan. Abraham's notion of sleeping with his wife's servant

Hagar tried to shortcut God's plan and His timetable for Sarah to conceive. David was tempted to kill Saul in a cave rather than patiently wait to become king. The Enemy loves to take a kernel of truth and twist and pervert it in such a way that you think you are expediting God's plan. But it is *never ok* to break God's law in order to achieve His goals. When we implement our own plan of action rather than seek His will and cling to His ways, the result is never what was truly intended by God in the first place.

God can and does, of course, make "beautiful things out of dust," as Gungor writes in his famous praise song. He can take the messy aftermath of your shortcuts and "work it for good, for those who love God and are called according to His purposes," as is promised in Romans 8:28. I know the pain, bad choices, disasters, and disappointments I've endured in my own life are being used for good today. They have shaped me into a more contrite and compassionate person. My heart is more open to following God. I try to fill it with the courage and boldness required for me to admit the failure of my own shortcuts in my confessional writing. In talking with others, I try to help them strive to achieve a life rich with purpose and meaning. If we follow God's directions to the letter, no matter how illogical or tedious they might seem to us, we can move closer to that goal every day.

Keys to Kingdom Living: Embrace God's way of doing things using His methods and following His timing.

Doorpost: "Don't look for shortcuts to God. The market is flooded with surefire, easy formulas for a successful life that can be practiced in your spare time. Don't fall for that stuff . . ." Matthew 7:13–14 (MSG)

TESTING 1, 2, 3: ENDING THE PREP AND TAKING THE TEST

*E*ven though shortcuts regarding God's plans can entrap a well-meaning follower, the trap of inaction is another snare we must guard against. This past summer, my son needed to take a series of placement tests to determine his math proficiency as he undertook the study of engineering. Initially, the call of summer fun beckoned and he ignored the long deadline ahead of him. Waiting until the last few weeks to begin to review and relearn some concepts, fear crept in that he would not do well and the procrastination continued. It was not until he was right up against the deadline that he took the test. He did not do as well as he might have if he had studied longer or not been as stressed. Even more regrettable is that he then had to take additional mini-classes, resulting in more overall work.

Sometimes we need to move against our fears and pull ourselves out of the inertia that can paralyze us from proactivity. I think sometimes Satan gets a foothold by inserting suggestions or concerns into our minds that lead to procrastination and run counter to God's plans. When Moses was face to face with the Red Sea, he was inclined to pray rather than move forward in faith. But there is a time for prayer and a time for action. When prayer is used to stall, it is not serving its intended purpose. So as God told Moses as recorded in Exodus 14:15, "Quit praying and get the people moving!" Forward, march!

Sometimes I find myself in a quandary over which situations require a quest for perfection and which of them might be hindered by a quest that may serve as more of an obstacle than an objective. Do the name tags for my gratitude brunch really need to be done by a calligrapher? Do I really need to go to three stores to look for just the right shade of ribbon for them? Do my Christmas cards need to be photoshopped to perfection? Often in our quest for perfection, we abandon the tasks altogether. The haunting of my mother's mantra is, "If you can't do it right, don't do it at all." For her, right was perfect.

Even though God is perfect, we are not. The perfect name tag is not a requirement for an atmosphere of expressing thanks to Him. The true meaning of Christmas is not diminished by the lack of a perfect Christmas card. Not every "ark" we build for God is going to require years of preparation. We can stop to pray with someone who is in tears without pausing to head over to church, offer confession, and then taking communion before returning to the task at hand. God's timing was in the prayer request in the first place; by initiating our own delay, we actually demonstrate our lack of trust in God.

This kind of inaction shows up in very common ways, such as the Christian who hasn't found the perfect church so they don't go at all. God wants us all in, right now, listening to Him. He's not interested in our "dog ate my homework" stories.

Keys to Kingdom Living: Listen for God's cues to move against your fears.

Doorpost: "Therefore, prepare your minds for action." 1 Peter 1:13 (NASB)

TESTING 1, 2, 3: CHECKING YOUR WORK

*O*ne of the hardest things about growing older is the sad realization that our memories and recollections are not infallible. Fortunately, a continual review of information through storytelling or research helps to ward off forgetfulness. When we are frustrated about wondering how a word might be spelled, for instance, we can search on the Internet for a handy refresher.

As we strive to live our lives to the glory of God, we can't rely on what we remember or have already learned about God from past readings or study classes. We have to continually study His Word. We need fresh reminders of His laws, His promises, and His eternal, amazing love! A parent can't expect a young child to ask forgiveness or thank God for dinner if they're only told once to do it and never again reminded them of it. We are never too old for reminders. In the test of Life and the paths we choose to take along the way, we check our work against what has been studied by generations of Christ-followers to determine whether we've properly applied our knowledge.

Only God is omniscient. There is no formulaic timetable for "getting" God, no certificate of completion—in this lifetime, anyway. I will never forget a story told by the oldest member in my Bible study. Friends often asked her why, in her early 80s, was she still attending after three-plus decades of doing so. "Well, I still don't know it all yet," she humbly replied. In fact, learning to live according to God's will is a lifetime endeavor. This undertaking won't be completed for any of us until the day the Lord takes us home to be with Him in paradise. How we spend our time between now and then will ultimately glorify or grieve Him.

Schedule choices always require challenging self-sacrifice. A rainy day tempts us to stay inside and skip Bible study. A perceived need for a manicure for haggard nails trumps a regular prayer meeting with friends. Skewed priorities can disrupt our once best-laid plans. But when we continually put our own plans ahead of spending time with God, we cause a break in relationship. Partnering with God in reflection and projection requires meeting regularly with Him to set our current and future goals. When we partner with other believers, we increase our chances of success through further commitment and accountability.

We can never fully measure up to God's standards on this side of eternity. But if we continue to take His tests, and check our work against His laws and precepts, we'll better know the difference between right and wrong, between disobedience and repentance. God needs to be our divine Proctor in this life so we can pass His test and make it to the next.

Keys to Kingdom Living: Check your life work to determine God's divine design for living.

Doorpost: "Your word is a lamp for my feet, a light on my path." Psalm 119:105

TESTING 1, 2, 3: NO CHEATING

*W*hen I was in college taking my Russian History exam, I remember sitting down to my desk, picking up my pencil, and suddenly seeing an unbelievable sight: the student in front of me was pulling back her sleeve to reveal a forearm of writing that today might be mistaken for a tattoo. On it, she had written the entire history of the Bolsheviks and the Cold War for her personal reference. I glanced at a friend in the class who had seen the same thing. We all sat for the exam and turned in our work at the end of the period

As we were leaving the classroom, my friend said we were obligated to tell the teacher what the student in front of us had done. When I hesitated, she reminded me that the test would be graded on a curve and that the student's grade, unfairly achieved, would impact our marks as well. I agreed to go to the professor with her and testify to what had happened. Justice was served.

Sadly, in today's world, people who have cheated and gotten away with embarrassing misdeeds and even serious crimes against humanity are celebrated on gossip shows. Accountability is sadly lacking in society. Who among us hasn't been in a situation where justice was not served? Maybe you've been a victim of a hit-and-run accident. Maybe your spouse owes child support and refuses to pay it while court systems do nothing to expedite a solution. Perhaps you lost a promotion to someone who took credit for an idea that was actually yours in the first place. Recently I tried to help out a friend whose car was totaled by attempting to locate an inexpensive used car in good condition. An acquaintance of mine, whom I have known for over a decade, told me how great her used car was, so I trusted her—and the car turned out to be a major lemon even as she denied its problems over and over again. Sadly, repair bills do not lie. I let it go, and I continually remind myself that God will even the score in His way and in His time. At the end of our lives, there will not be any way to "cheat" to get into heaven any more than we will be able to "cheat" death. Our Righteous Judge sees and knows all. His eyes "move to and fro throughout the earth that He may strongly support those whose hearts are completely His," we read in 2 Chronicles 16:9. Thankfully, we can count on Him to right the wrongs without taking vigilante justice into our own hands.

When I feel the scales are unbalanced, I remind myself of this verse from Joel 2:25: "I will repay you for the years the locusts have eaten [your crops]." We can trust God to keep that promise, just as we can rest in knowing that our fellow eternity dwellers who will walk among us will not have cheated their way into the pearly gates.

Keys to Kingdom Living: Trust God to right all wrongs.

Doorpost: "So if you have not been trustworthy in handling worldly wealth, who will trust you with true riches? . . . No one can serve two masters." Luke 16:11–13

TESTING 1, 2, 3: TUTORING AND
BEING TUTORED

*G*etting high school students prepped for the ACT and SAT is a big business these days. Tutoring programs designed to optimize their scores abound online and in our local communities. The tutors themselves are often graduate students, possessing credentials so impressive parents are attracted to the implied promise that their own child should only fare so well. Some of them received similar tutoring in order to position them for their individual launchpads of success.

As you navigate your spiritual journeys, seek out people who can "prep" you for eternity. As we foster and enjoy a mentor beyond our years, we too should identify someone younger to give a leg up, so to speak, as they embark on their journey.

Rich examples of these relationships abound in the Bible. Moses mentored Aaron in the wilderness as they served God and ministered to the Israelites. Paul mentored Timothy, leaving in his epistles many verses outlining mentoring benefits. In 2 Timothy 2:2 we read, "The things which you have heard from me in the presence of many witnesses, entrust these to faithful men who will be able to teach others also."

The Bible mentions mentoring for women. In Titus 2:3–4 we read that older women should embrace sober living and refrain from gossip, being "reverent in their behavior . . . Teaching what is good so that they may encourage the young women to love their husbands, to love their children." Though many of us parents are naturally mentoring our children and training them in the ways of the Lord, our duty is not limited only to them. We can, and should, continue to encourage, nurture, and equip the next generation to carry on the good fight until the day Jesus Christ returns.

The blessings connected with mentoring are so far-reaching and numerous that this page couldn't hold them all. When we are ideally mentored, we benefit from someone with more life experience as a Christ-follower. They have encountered their share of hurdles, are serving God actively, and are mentored by someone older than them as well. No one is above being mentored. Pastor and author Rick Warren counted Billy Graham as one of his mentors, and he has spoken often about meeting with him whenever their schedules permitted.

Perhaps the best case for mentoring was made by Jesus when He laid out the many ways our ministering to others is "done unto Him." I often think of how I could have avoided countless mistakes in my life, had I had a truly caring and involved spiritual mentor. Fortunately, God never wastes a hurt. I now offer wisdom and encouragement to teens about walking closely with God. I recently saw this quote on my Facebook feed: "Be who you needed when you were younger." Ruminate on this truth and ask God to reveal a mentor or mentee to you; your life will be enriched in many ways.

Keys to Kingdom Living: Seek and provide encouragement in your life journey.

Doorpost: "As iron sharpens iron, so one person sharpens another." Proverbs 27:17

TESTING 1, 2, 3: THE PASS/FAIL OF SALVATION

*M*uch is made in today's culture about shades of grey. Satan loves the notion of grey and wants you to embrace it, too. He delights in the idea that to sin or not to sin is more complicated than the white of purity or the black of dark deeds and desires that run contrary to God's laws. From the moment Eve bit into the fruit, Satan has been trying to taint the white of obedience with drops of black.

We continually see these notions sugar-coated to make them more "palatable" as popular opinion and political correctness eat away at society's moral fiber. Stick it to the man by hooking up illegal cable. Download music illegally, like everyone else. How bad can it be if everyone is doing it? These, and other ideas like them, contribute to a slippery slope in today's society.

Nothing in God's Word backs up the notion of grey as neutral ground between right and wrong. When it comes to the left hand of God versus the right, the destination is as black and white as they come. At the end of time, you will either be with the sheep or the goats, as we are told in Matthew 25:32. "When the Son of Man comes in His glory, and all the angels with Him, He will sit on His glorious throne. All the nations will be gathered before Him, and He will separate the people one from another as a shepherd separates the sheep from the goats. He will put the sheep on His right and the goats on His left."

Even though we do not earn our salvation with good works or deeds, God's grace is, in one way, a pass/fail system. We are given a redemptive pass when we repent of our wrongdoing and accept Jesus Christ and His grace into our hearts, entering into relationship with Him. Those who neglect to do this fail to redeem themselves and are destined to an eternity that excludes them from God's permanent presence and fails to restore them to right relationship with God. We are told in Matthew 7, verses 13 and 14, to enter "by the narrow gate. For the gate that is wide and the way that is easy leads to destruction, and those who enter by it are many. For the gate is narrow and way is hard that leads to life, and those who find it are few." The narrow and wide gates both lead to eternity, but the narrow gate is a pass to Jesus while the wide gate fails to lead us to God and instead directs those who pass through it to the torment of permanent separation from God.

Our pass or fail status is determined by the gate we choose to enter. When college students elect to take a pass/fail class, they can retake the class to try to better learn the material in order to pass it. But we won't have a chance for a do-over in life. We have but one to live on this earth to choose to live eternally with Jesus Christ.

Keys to Kingdom Living: We all choose to be sheep or goats and must accept the pass/fail grade we will earn.

Doorpost: "Or do you not know that the unrighteous will not inherit the kingdom of God?" 1 Corinthians 6:9 (ESV)

WEEK 6: CONSISTENCY

CONSISTENCY IN OUR WALK
OF FAITH

I remember the first time I took my oldest to Disneyland. He was just a little under two years old. His eyes were as wide as saucers when we floated through the It's a Small World ride. His mouth hung open as the Disney characters marched in the afternoon parade. He tilted back his little head to take in the amazing fireworks show when darkness came. Today my son is twenty-two. He has probably been to Disneyland more than 200 times, so it's probably safe to say he's a bit jaded about the park after so many visits. It is hard to say if he would venture through the gates if I handed him a free ticket. At the moment, this thrill is gone.

The sheer joy and excitement of a person who is freshly devoted to the Lord is as exciting to be around as it is contagious. Such an individual has just experienced a game-changing event in their life. They have found their hope and are eager to share their joy and story of their personal embrace of the Christian life. They retell the moment they saw the light, what it continues to mean to them today, and they are anxious to tell others less convinced about what it can mean in their lives.

An effective walk with the Lord involves more than an emotional response to His grace and mercy, however. It involves consistent response. Few people, if any, can sustain such an emotional high for any extended length of time. God's prophets have spoken of these dry spells over the years. In Psalm 10:1, David writes, "Why, Lord, do you stand far away?" God is, of course, never far away from us. "I will never leave you or forsake you," He promises in Deuteronomy 1:6. The antidote for these so-called dry periods is to stay on God's path by simply continuing to walk on it. We put one foot in front of the other, knowing that His holy Word is "a lamp unto our feet and a light unto our path." You can't just take one step and expect to get anywhere. We take one step, and then the next, and only then can we make any real headway.

Sometimes we need to take a step back and view the full picture. God may have designed this seemingly dry period for purposes of reflection or to get us ready for the next plan and purpose He has in mind. Or the feeling of dryness may stem from an unrealistic expectation. Reality TV shows fuel this fire of requiring "big reveals" or zenith moments. God is not required to provide these for your daily sustenance. He wants our obedience and faithfulness regardless of our emotional state.

A.W. Tozer said, "Feeling is the play of emotions over will, the will, a kind of musical accompaniment to the business of living. And while it is indeed most enjoyable to have the band play as we march to Zion, it's by no means indispensable. We can work and walk without music and, if we have true faith, we can walk with God without feeling."

Keys to Kingdom Living: Listen for God's leading in zenith faith moments and dry spells.

Doorpost: "Keep this Book of the Law always on your lips; meditate on it day and night, so that you may be careful to do everything written in it. Then you will be prosperous and successful." Joshua 1:8

CONSISTENCY IN THE GIVING AND
RECEIVING OF GRACE

*G*od's free gift of grace, made possible through the redemptive blood of Jesus Christ, reads on paper like a simple concept. All we need to do is simply accept it and, in turn, dispense it when the occasion requires. Yet, like so many other areas of obedience to God, temptations and traps sometimes prevent us from experiencing its immediate benefits.

One of the most common obstacles involves the notion that we are not worthy of God's grace. We might tell ourselves that what we have done is just too unforgivable. The Enemy will do everything in his power to enable this belief, but it simply isn't true. Jesus forgave the thief on the cross. He restored Watergate criminal Charles Colson, filled him with the Holy Spirit, and even raised him up to be a great prison minister. He forgave a penitent David, who is referred to as "A man after God's own heart" in Acts 13:22. He will forgive and restore you and me completely and consistently when we come before Him with a sincerely repentant heart.

The posture of our hearts is in direct correlation to the posture of our pride. When our pride runs amok, we sit up a little too straight and tall, sporting an arrogantly raised chin and an even stiffer upper lip. We may say, "I will never forgive so-and-so for what they said and did to me." Those words and that attitude build a wall between the heart and the head to such a degree that the heart is rendered flat and inoperative.

Sometimes, the opposite is true. Our hearts grieve over a terrible sin we have committed. Our hearts balloon in this grief, and they crowd out all the promises made by our Kinsman-Redeemer that are present in our minds. This state of the heart, left unchecked, can prevent us from receiving the grace already won on the cross by Him. Grace not dispensed, as well as grace not received, is the unopened gift we need to open or hand off to others every day.

We are told in Proverbs 4:23 to guard our heart because it is "the wellspring of life." When we fail to internalize God's gift of grace, we prevent ourselves from "renewing a right spirit within us," as we are told in Psalm 51:10. Likewise, we are to dispense grace and even forgive those who have not asked for forgiveness as Jesus did on the cross when He spoke the first of seven utterances on the cross: "Father forgive them, for they know not what they do," (Luke 23:34). When we do not forgive, the penalty is steep. Jesus said in Matthew 6:15, "But if you do not forgive others their sins, your Father will not forgive your sins." We are bound as children of Christ Jesus to continually repent and allow ourselves to be restored, just as we must forgive and restore our earthly relationships. We must suppress our pride and express our forgiveness.

Keys to Kingdom Living: God's grace must be both freely received and dispensed.

Doorpost: "Do not condemn, and you will not be condemned. Forgive, and you will be forgiven." Luke 6:37

CONSISTENCY WITH REGARD TO HONESTY

One afternoon a neighbor came to my door and said she had seen a neighbor teen on his bike ride by one of my cars and smash the door in with his fist, leaving a permanent dent in the car. I walked over to his house on the corner and his mother answered the door. I told her what had been relayed to me, so she called him into the room and asked him about it. When he looked me right in the eye and denied the story, his mother said, "My son has never lied to me before, so I believe him now."

My mouth hung open as I left their house. A teenager who had never lied to his parents was almost as unbelievable as a mom who would tell such a bold-faced lie in front of her teenager in order to save his skin. I took my indignation and filed it away under the "God will someday right every wrong" category.

Stories of children lying and deceiving fill the Bible as well as volumes of childhood literature. In Genesis 4:9, Adam and Eve's son Cain lied to God about not knowing where Abel was, even though he had killed him earlier when they were out in the field. And Jacob participated in the deception of Isaac in receiving the blessing intended for Esau. In Carlo Collodi's 1883 book *Pinocchio*, we are told of the puppet whose nose grows longer every time he lies. If only life were like that, and we could determine who is telling the truth to us. Then again, who among us would not be a candidate for rhinoplasty? (That's doctor talk for nose job!) Our honesty must be complete.

Lapses in honesty in our society at large may not be obvious to us as the Pinocchio scenario. But God sees and knows everything. We're called to stop lying to one another and put off the old life in Colossians 3:9. And we're certainly commanded not to bear false witness against our neighbors, as recorded in Exodus. Though we tend to categorize our lies into degrees of severity, there are no "white lies" to God any more than some sins are less grievous. If we lie and say "the check is in the mail," it is just as grievous to God as the Boston Marathon bombing.

The best way to ward off dishonesty is to remind ourselves how lies erode our resolve for obedience and open the door to more lies. Often a lie must be retold—or, better yet, admitted and corrected. His Word is our best defense against lies. In The Message Bible, we are told in Colossians 3:15–17 to let God's Word "have the run of the house. Give it plenty of room in your lives . . . Let every detail in your lives—words, actions, whatever —be done in the name of the Master." When we mess up, we must quickly ask for forgiveness, return to God, follow His edicts, and uphold the honesty He demands. Pray for consistency with regard to your personal honesty.

Keys to Kingdom Living: We must continually guard our words and actions to reflect honest living.

Doorpost: "The integrity of the upright guides them, but the unfaithful are destroyed by their duplicity." Proverbs 11:3

CONSISTENCY IN REMAINING IN COMMUNITY

*T*oday's technology in bringing worship and the Word to God's people solves problems . . . but also creates new ones. Never before have such a variety of worship service options been available for shut-ins and the incarcerated. Television programs, podcasts, live feeds, radio programs, recorded books and more are available at the click of a mouse.

But another thing it has done is given people a reason to avoid the community of believers. We can squeeze in listening to the message on a CD in the car while we are driving. We can curl up with a blanket and our hot beverage and buttery pastries and listen to a podcast. While there in nothing inherently wrong in occasionally doing this due to sickness or schedule conflicts, when able-bodied people neglect to meet in person with fellow believers in community, it runs contrary to God's plan for His people.

There are two reasons why we must never fully isolate ourselves from other believers: it poses risks for even the strongest Christian and it runs contrary to the plans and purposes God has for us as His servants. In Genesis 2:18, God says, "It is not good for man to be alone." When we are alone, we have no one to bounce off our ideas or test what we are thinking against truth and perspective. We read in Proverbs 18:1 that one who isolates himself rejects all sound judgment. In

Ecclesiastes we read in 4:9, "Two people are better off than one, for they can help each other succeed. If one person falls, the other can help. But someone who falls alone is in real trouble" (NLT).

When I was a kid, I was fascinated by the B-rate African explorer movies of the '60s, especially when people fell into quicksand. You don't hear about quicksand much today, but it is defined as "loose, wet sand that yields easily to pressure and sucks in anything resting on or falling into it." In these films, someone often seemed to be lagging behind and falling into it, never to be seen or heard from again. I remember thinking: in a jungle full of danger, why would anyone separate himself from the group? If someone stepped in quicksand, then the group could work together to rescue him from a sure death.

Our world is dangerous and full of quicksand. Many—maybe even you—are perishing. Some are so despondent they're convinced they can't escape their quicksand. Some don't cry for help at all and just sink into oblivion. If we don't put ourselves in community to help seek out and save the lost, is the love of God really in us?

Keys to Kingdom Living: Meet other believers in community to consistently receive and provide encouragement.

Doorpost: "And let us consider how we may spur one another on toward love and good deeds, not giving up meeting together, as some are in the habit of doing, but encouraging one another." Hebrews 10:24–25

CONSISTENCY WITH QUIET TIME

*M*uch is made of the so-called mountaintop experiences with God. You may have experienced a quiet time when God spoke and ministered to you in an exhilarating way, leaving you as elevated as a helium balloon and so full of joy you felt as if you might burst.

But if you are faithful in your quiet time, meeting with the Lord daily (as you might be doing now with this book), you know that your daily encounters with God are not going to necessarily leave you "feeling" full of helium. I spent most of my life entrapped in a feelings-driven existence until I was able to break free from those bonds and cling instead to truth and promises rather than emotions. The truth—of God and who He is and all He has promised—has indeed set me free (John 8:32), and I am no longer a slave to emotion.

Quiet time with God needs to be consistent. When it is, it will be characterized by mountaintop mornings intermingled with less emotive but nevertheless productive times spent with Him. Systematically internalizing God's Word fills up your reservoir for use on a dry day sure to come your way in the future. The lack of an emotional high in quiet time is not indicative of its effectiveness.

I remember one year I was feeling particularly deflated. Alone and unchecked with my negative thoughts, I experienced a season of paranoia. My people-pleasing existence kept me from fully enjoying the depth of God's love and recognizing that His love is criticial to achieving spiritual fulfillment. One day as I was reading my Bible, I began to meditate on the beautiful truths in Ephesians 3:17–18: "And I pray that you, being rooted and established in love, may have power, together with all the Lord's holy people, to grasp how wide and long and high and deep is the love of Christ." Though I had seen it many times before, this time the words seem to leap off the page in front of me.

I resolved then and there to meditate on those verses frequently, quietly, and consistently. I taped a printout of them to my medicine cabinet, wrote it in my study book, and marked it in my iPad. I made it my prayer for a year that, with God's help, I would internalize His perfect love. I'm here to tell you that this prayer was answered. Whenever a seemingly insurmountable emotion of unworthiness comes over me, I remind myself that I am a daughter of the King! His love for me is all I need to face life's daily challenges.

When I look back on two decades of studying God's Word, I can't honestly say I have instant recall and optimum application of every verse. What I can say is that my overall faithfulness to persevere in study and meditate on these truths has built up a wellspring of God's wisdom that I would not have been able to cultivate any other way. If I had simply amassed a handful of mountaintop experiences without the benefit of daily bread, spiritual malnutrition would have set in.

Keys to Kingdom Living: Persevere to read and apply God's truth with consistency.

Doorpost: "They rose early in the morning and worshiped before the Lord." 1 Samuel 1:19 (ESV)

CONSISTENCY IN SERVICE TO GOD

*F*riends who grew up in service-oriented families love to tell tales of their early taste of service to society and their Servant King. Their parents modeled and encouraged giving back to the community and assisting the marginalized. They love to testify about how it shaped them to continue the family tradition they spearhead today with their own children.

My parents were passionate in their situational giving but less consistent in its structure. My mother would dive into the occasional project to help others when a need presented itself. She once invited a family to our house for Christmas when the father lost his job. This had an impact on my compassion for children who do not receive Christmas gifts, and I remember this every year when my son and I participate in Franklin Graham's Operation Christmas Child.

As the co-head of my own house, I vowed to stress systematic service as part of being a good steward of both time and resources in my immediate family. My husband and I often accompanied our older son to feed the homeless, repair dilapidated public housing, and work food and clothing drives. When he was older, he began serving on his own in Mexico, building houses for a sweat-equity non-profit. Because it was modeled for him consistently, it was easier for him to cultivate a heart of his own for society's marginalized. I believe he will remember and carry on this tradition in his own family one day because it was modeled in his family of origin.

The structure providing this consistency today is our couples life group. The eight of us, with a teen or two occasionally in tow, partner with local organizations and ink in dates, times, and projects like driving for a local meal delivery service, so that at least one service project is always on our calendar. This keeps us accountable to our service goals and allows local organizations to know they can depend on us to plan our service and show up to actually do it.

While spontaneous service meets the needs of the recipient, systematic service takes sacrificial giving to a higher level. When we're consistent in our service, we honor God by imitating Christ. Our life and its structure is reflective of His priorities. Jesus spelled out these priorities in Matthew 28:20, saying, "Just as the Son of Man did not come to be served but to be served and give His life as a ransom for many."

When we serve with a fully engaged heart as an imitator of Christ, we are reminded of all that Christ did for us—and, in turn, our sacrifice is a joyful offering of gratitude.

Keys to Kingdom Living: Systematic service to the marginalized blesses others, yourself, and God.

Doorpost: "In view of God's mercy . . . offer your bodies as a living sacrifice, holy and pleasing to God." Romans 12:1

CONSISTENCY IN OUR PRAYER LIFE

*O*nce when my brother was small, he was in the garage hovering over a hammer and a piece of wood. My dad was observing him from the driveway. My brother's eyes were closed and his grip on the hammer was tight. My dad walked in and asked him if anything was wrong. My brother told him that he was praying hard that he would not hurt himself hammering.

Young or old, Christian or agnostic, people from all walks of life offer up emergency prayers when in a scrape or faced with paralyzing fear or crisis. But the sincere, heartfelt, non-rote daily prayers of those who devote themselves to intimately talking with God consistently lay the groundwork for something much deeper and more valuable. If our prayer life consists primarily of the "arrow prayer," or the petition offered up in crisis, we are much like the child who only communicates with his parents to get something he wants.

True relationship is based on more than just a presentation of a Christmas list. When we are facing monumental, seemingly unsolvable circumstances, we aren't likely to dial up someone we met the day before. We're more inclined to pour our heart out to someone who's known us inside and out for many years. Even though God hears our prayers and knows our needs before we say or do anything, He wants us to desire relationship with Him.

We accomplish this best by engaging in regular communication with Him throughout our day.

I remember once hearing some tips on what prayer time actually looks like in a 21st-century life. One of my mentors shared with the group how she likes to start her day with God and end it in the same way. In the morning, she prays to be effective during the day and responsive to the needs of others. She also said she takes time to petition for others, as well as for herself, those things heavy on her heart and mind. At the end of the day, she shared how it's important to go before the Lord to check in about her efforts and cover anything new that may have occurred, as well as preparing for the coming day by lifting up any other appropriate concerns.

Exactly what your prayer time looks like from a structural viewpoint will in part depend on your season of life. The young mom with six kids may not be able to carve out the same time every day and night to pray the way a woman in her seventies, with an empty nest, can. But the desire should remain strong. Structure is important but should not hinder our efforts. Consider the wisdom imparted in 1 Samuel 16:7: "Man looks on the outer appearance, but the Lord looks at the heart." A life devoted to intimate communiqué with God enriches us and pleases Him.

Keys to Kingdom Living: Gravitate to consistent prayer without continually relying on emergency mode.

Doorpost: "Rejoice always, pray without ceasing, give thanks in all circumstances; for this is the will of God in Christ Jesus for you." 1 Thessalonians 5:16–18

WEEK 7: CURTAIN CALL

CURTAIN CALL: ON THE SEPARATION FROM GOD

*B*ack in my fashion reporter days when I covered the red carpet arrivals at the Oscars, I had to jump through hoops to receive the proper credentials. This paperwork had to be filled out months in advance. I had to wear laminated badges and special pins to gain access to the highly coveted positions. From 2 – 5 p.m. I was permitted to stand near the red runner, but once 5 p.m. rolled around, my access ended. I was not permitted to pass through the curtain into the building where the awards were presented.

The early church hierarchy also operated on a system of exclusivity. Only high priests were permitted behind the curtain to enter the holy of holies on one day each year. Anyone unauthorized who tried to enter perished immediately. (The deaths of Aaron's two sons recorded in Leviticus 10 were caused by such a breach.) The reason for this separation is spelled out in Isaiah 59 of The Message: "Your wrongheaded lives caused the split between you and God." The curtain would only be removed by the sacrifice of the unblemished Lamb after He made atonement for our sins.

On the day Jesus Christ was crucified and redeemed us from the pit, the inner curtain of the temple was torn in two. We read in Matthew 27:50 that when Jesus cried out in a loud voice to give up His spirit, "At that moment the curtain was torn in two from top to bottom." As contemporary Christians, we can't appreciate the impact of the significance of that curtain being torn, but God was signifying that His people were no longer bound to follow the elaborate ceremonial law recorded for pages on end in Leviticus. They were no longer condemned for their inability to perfectly keep God's ten commandments. From then on, everyone destined to put their faith in Jesus Christ was filled with Him, becoming the temples of God He had originally intended. Paul writes in Hebrews 10:19 about how we no longer need a priest to intercede between us and God, but that we can boldly approach His throne of grace—and no holy place, even heaven, will be off limits for those who love the Lord and invite Him into their hearts.

Modern-day Christian women cannot fully appreciate what the removal meant to those back in the day. Women traditionally weren't permitted inside certain areas of the temple and were not allowed to participate in any ceremonies held in the synagogue. Women did not receive any instruction from great rabbis of the day and weren't allowed to teach spiritual matters. We should give unending thanks to God for the full scope of what He has done in removing the curtain and securing our restoration.

Keys to Kingdom Living: Give thanks to Jesus for paying the ultimate price to bring down the curtain.

Doorpost: "I will make a covenant of peace with them, an everlasting covenant. . . . I will make my home among them. I will be their God, and they will be my people." Ezekiel 37:26–27 (NLT)

CURTAIN CALL: ESTABLISHING ALL ACCESS

*E*xclusivity and elite status monikers are important commodities in today's consumer world. Marketing gurus know that the more special a customer feels, the more inclined the customer is to foster loyalty. Who can even keep up with comically high number of loyalty levels for the airlines?

Visible status symbols of these membership levels are everywhere. The Visa Black card (with a fee of almost $500 per year), the "key" to the private club, or the ring or pin that signifies we belong, all indirectly communicate economic or power status whenever flashed in public.

Ironically, the most elite enclave touting the best benefits, personal attention, and highest satisfaction is non-exclusive. It's available to all, not fee-based or even performance-based. It's membership in God's forever family. Unlike the clubs on earth that require special skills, dues, or demand certain physical attributes, membership in God's family centers around God's free gift of grace for those who believe in the power of the cross. We read in John 10:28 that to those who believe God promises "eternal life, and they shall never perish; no one will snatch them out of my hand."

People truly belonging to God receive the inimitable distinction of having their names written in the Book of Life by God himself. Unlike elite earthly clubs, Bible verses like the one found in John 10 support the fact that once these individual's names are written in the Book, they're permanently grafted into God's family. Membership benefits in God's family are also without expiration dates. We receive a sealed adoption by our Father God. We're told in 2 Corinthians 1:21–22 that we are established in Christ and that He has "put His seal on us and given us His Spirit in our hearts as a guarantee." We are His heirs in every sense of that word. We will "share in the inheritance of the saints in light," as promised in Colossians 1:12. In 1 Corinthians 2:9, we read that "no eye has seen, no ear has heard, no heart has imagined, what God has prepared for those who love him." What a promise!

We also receive the peace of mind that comes from God's promises. We read in Romans 5:1 that "since we have been justified by faith, we have peace with God through our Lord Jesus Christ." Finally, we have an expanded family of fellow members to enjoy here on earth and a host of others, the "family of believers" mentioned in Galatians 6:10, whom we will meet and enjoy in heaven someday. Imagine that membership roster!

Unlike many earthly clubs with restricted velvet rope and curtain barriers, we can enjoy all-access in the heavenly realm one day. Now, the only curtain that may stand between you and God is one of your own making. Tear it down today.

Keys to Kingdom Living: Open your heart to Jesus and begin enjoying all access.

Doorpost: "And I will be your Father, and you will be my sons and daughters." 2 Corinthians 6:18 (NLT)

CURTAIN CALL: MAN-MADE BARRIERS
TO GOD

*M*y mother played the accordion for many years. It always amazed me how the little folds between one side of the instrument and the other contracted and expanded to the extent they did. How interesting it would be to see how the makers of the instrument manage to precisely fold the soft middle to create a space where beautiful music can be made.

Our souls are like the middle of the accordion. When in the wrong hands, the middle is simply full of hot air, stretched out and not engaged with any thought as to a next step of any kind. Those who don't belong to Jesus—and even some of us who do —erect layers of "folds" between themselves and God, often without even realizing it.

Some of these folds are emotional, like the notion that you're unworthy of following God due to past sins and general imperfection. Or maybe bitterness has taken root because of unimaginable tragedies and injustice. Sometimes the folds are more circumstantial in nature. Sunday morning sporting events might take precedence over being in God's presence on the Sabbath, beginning a gradual move away from that commitment. Or the idea that Sunday is a catch-up day for your to-do list and that church will have to wait another week. Then the quiet time you mean to have is interrupted by a text that leads into a phone call followed up with checking emails and playing

Words with Friends . . . until suddenly it's afternoon and your kids are walking through the door.

Regardless of what causes the folds, our hands need to compress them. We need to make sure the hot air is squeezed out of our soul "instruments" so they are ready to make "a joyful noise," as David wrote in Psalm 100. The message spells it out beautifully in 2 Corinthians 10:3–6: "We use our powerful God tools for smashing warped philosophies, [and] tearing down barriers erected against the truth of God" (MSG).

Tearing down these walls and barriers requires tenacity, perseverance, courage, and—most of all—God's help. The encouraging words from Jeremiah 29:13, that "you will seek Me and find Me when you seek Me with all of your heart," reinforce the idea that God honors our desire to commune with Him. That is not to say that the Enemy won't throw up every potential obstacle in his power to keep you from doing just that. He loves nothing more than looking at a sea of stretched-out accordions quietly gathering dust.

Keys to Kingdom Living: By keeping our hands on the game, our eyes on the prize, and offering petitions for help, we keep our instruments actively compressed and ready for faithful devotion and service.

Doorpost: "For He himself is our peace, who has . . . destroyed the barrier, the dividing wall of hostility." Ephesians 2:14

CURTAIN CALL: WHEN IT'S TIME FOR
YOU TO CLOSE DOWN THE OLD ACT

*B*eginning in July of 1971, Broadway theatergoers have been watching *The Phantom of the Opera* on New York's Broadway stages. To date it remains the longest-running show on Broadway. But prior to that, *Hello, Dolly!* held the proud distinction.

With the exception of our salvation and the relationships God blesses, most of the possessions and relationships we enjoy at various times in our lives will have expiration dates. You probably don't see all of your elementary school classmates on a daily basis. You don't sleep with the stuffed bunny your grandmother gave you when you were two. It's unlikely you will drive your very first car well into your adult years.

We are told in Ecclesiastes 3:1, "To everything there is a season, and a time to every purpose under the heaven." When we give our lives to Christ, Paul tells us in Ephesians 4:22–24, we are to "put off your old self which belongs to your former manner of life . . . and to put on the new self, created after the likeness of God in true righteousness and holiness" (ESV). If you suffer from addiction, that may mean closing the curtain on things in your drawers or cabinets. Or it may mean ridding yourself of companions who might thwart your faith-walk.

For some of us, especially those who revere loyalty as an important character trait, the idea of "unfriending" someone is contrary to our nature. We are indeed charged with bringing the good news to all people in Matthew 28. But the recovering alcoholic may not be strong enough to try to bring the good news to the homeless man on the street with a bottle in his hand. And a woman who suffers from shopaholic disorders should probably not pass out tracts in the shopping mall. We want to surround ourselves with companions who will bring us up higher, but when we're strong enough for service, we also want to be ready to get our hands dirty. We need to use discernment and ask God for wisdom when we consider who we spend time with and, more importantly, why.

Certainly, love should be the primary motivating factor in all our relationships. We need to love others enough to help bring them into the fold. We should be persistent but realistic in prayer about where we are. Good advice regarding this is offered in Matthew 10:14: "If anyone will not welcome you or listen to your words, leave that home or town and shake the dust off your feet."

Keys to Kingdom Living: Seek God's direction before pulling the curtain, but be bold enough to do so when necessary.

Doorpost: "Let us throw off everything that hinders and the sin that so easily entangles." Hebrews 12:1

CURTAIN CALL: BACKSTAGE
SABOTAGE AND OTHER OBSTACLES

*B*ack in the vaudeville days, stage managers were equipped with long canes called hooks, and they were used backstage to physically—and not very subtly—remove stage performers who were not delighting their audiences. When someone was physically removed from the stage, it was referred to as "getting the hook." You may have seen old shows where the performers tried to fight the hook, by going around it to get back on stage even as others were trying to remove them. Their love of the stage kept them on, even if the response was less than stellar.

When we are trying to win people for Jesus, we encounter a variety of "hooks" as well. Even though God wants His people restored even more than we want to win our friends for Christ, Satan is always backstage with his hook. He wants to interrupt God's program at all costs. He'll even dispense hooks to other bystanders in an effort to undermine our kingdom work. He wants to hook the person trying just to live for Jesus as well as the people who are toiling in the mission field.

Because he's so wily, he even sometimes manages to dispense an unwanted hook in our hands. This can happen to Christians even as they are working for Jesus. The driver with the "Not Of This World" bumper sticker might cut someone off on the way to Bible study: voila! He is carrying a hook. So is the married pastor who preaches on adultery from the pulpit on Sunday, only to meet up with his girlfriend on Monday.

Some hooks are more intentional than others. Satan's hooks are directly malicious, even as ours sometimes sneak up on us. But the effect is the same: someone is hindered from entering into the full presence of God. We're accountable when our walk doesn't match our talk. We read in 2 Timothy 2:15 that we are to do our best to represent ourselves as approved workmen who are unashamed of the gospel.

We want to make sure our aroma is pleasing to others so they will be attracted to God and the eternal life of peace and joy He offers. We want our hands to be so occupied with God's stage directions that we don't have room for hooks. By keeping busy and staying focused, we're less likely to find ourselves carrying hooks. When our hands are free to work, we are in a position to shine and not tarnish what God wants to produce and polish.

Keys to Kingdom Living: As God's ambassadors working the onstage mission field, we must be free from what entangles us to be effective.

Doorpost: "The good man out of the good treasure of his heart brings forth what is good; and the evil man out of the evil treasure brings forth what is evil; for his mouth speaks from that which fills his heart." Luke 6:45 (NASB)

CURTAIN CALL: ACKNOWLEDGING
OUR MORTALITY AND LIVING
ACCORDINGLY

*O*n February 17, 1673, playwright Moliere was acting a part in his comedic work, *The Imaginary Invalid*. He played the role of the hypochondriac. Toward the end of the final scene of the play, Moliere was seized by a fit of choking. Determined the show would go on, he finished the scene and took his bows without anyone realizing the choking event wasn't part of the play. Finally, once he was offstage, he was carried home, where he died within hours of the last act. None of the theatergoers knew what had transpired until well after the fact, any more than he knew when the play started that that would be his final curtain call—in every sense of the word.

As Christians, we know we will experience a curtain call of our own here on this side of eternity, but thankfully we do not have to fear it. We only have a finite amount of time here on Earth, a number which varies widely but will only extend ten decades or so at best. While we don't want to live like a hypochondriac, we should be mindful that our time here is as limited as it is unpredictable.

Why be mindful of something some people consider morbid? We need to be good stewards with our time. Time is a gift from God. It's not to be squandered away. He has entrusted a certain number of days for our use. We can wake up every day and spend our time glorifying Him and doing the things He's planned out for us, or we can indulge our own selfish pursuits by including God as an afterthought or occupier of our leftover time. Furthermore, by being mindful of our mortality, we're essentially reminding ourselves we are continually on standby for our departure. This impacts our thought life, our level of peace, and our general demeanor.

Likewise, we should not have a doomsday attitude. We can't walk around like a sad sack, complaining and ignoring doctor's orders. On the flip side, we don't jump out of planes without parachutes, assuming God has our back. We simply remind ourselves that, as Paul put it in Philippians 1:6, "He who began a good work in you will carry it on to completion until the day of Jesus Christ." You can't see God's to-do list for your life, but once it's completed you'll draw your last breath.

Jesus served as the ultimate model for pre-curtain-call living. He was at peace when the time came and willingly walked to Golgotha. He was not afraid to die—and neither should we be if we are Christians. Finally, He knew where He was going and trusted His Father's plan even in His darkest hour. When it comes to mortality, what looks like the final curtain call is simply an intermission.

Keys to Kingdom Living: Remain mindful of living each moment for God.

Doorpost: "I have fought the good fight, I have finished the course, I have kept the faith." 2 Timothy 4:7 (NASB)

CURTAIN CALLS: NO ENCORES

The encore in musical performances dates back to the 19th century when it was common for a piece of music to be replayed since recorded music was still unavailable. Over time, the encore was somewhat assimilated into the structure and time frame of a performance to such an extent that today the encore song is often a favorite, long anticipated from the moment the concert begins.

The protocol to summon an encore at rock concerts has evolved. In the '60s and '70s, concertgoers stamped their feet or flashed their lighters to signify the desire for more performance time. Nowadays, people hold up cell phones to illuminate the room. Whether or not an encore occurs is usually the performer's call, but some, like the legendary Elvis Presley, never did encores. He instructed his manager to blare out white noise through the speakers, and then utter the now popular phrase, "Elvis has left the building."

Inarguably the greatest encore in history was that of Jesus Christ, who after three days was resurrected from the dead. It's an encore no one has yet been able to top, no matter how many curtain calls they enjoy, how much applause is generated, or how many lighters or phones illuminate the stage. His return did not center on popular demand or the need for attention and approval. It was done out of obedience to His Father and love for us, as people "have sinned and fall short of the glory of God" (Romans 3:23). Unlike the non-spontaneous encores of the modern age, the encore of Jesus Christ generated an elation, devotion, and subsequent following that remains unmatched in every way in human history. Our Redeemer lives and reigns.

When we, like Elvis, leave life's building, we won't be weighing the options of an encore. No matter how many applaud or light a candle in our absence, we will not be able to reappear and begin again. We've but one life on this earth. We have the blessed assurance of heaven or the dismal prospect of eternal damnation. Whatever we do here will be examined and tested from the judgment seat when Jesus Christ comes again in glory. We can't put off until tomorrow what we can do today; we don't know what tomorrow will bring, or if we have tomorrow at all.

As we live life, we should never give credence to the notion that we have time to serve the Lord later. We can let all kinds of white noise get in the way of what God wants us to be doing (as opposed to what we are actually doing). In Isaiah 6:8 the prophet speaks of when he heard "the voice of the Lord saying, 'Whom shall I send, and who will go for us?'" "Here I am, send me!" Isaiah said. May that be our response each and every day.

Keys to Kingdom Living: Live every day to serve Jesus as if it's your last.

Doorpost: "Our days on earth are as fleeting as a shadow." Job 8:9 (NLT)

WEEK 8: THE CROSS

THE CROSS: WHAT JESUS WAS BORN
TO ENDURE AND EMBRACE

*A*rguably the most famous line in Frank Capra's 1946 movie *It's a Wonderful Life* is George Bailey's desperate utterance, "I wish I'd never been born at all." Of course, an angel and an alternate existence scenario convince Jimmy Stewart's character to not only resume but embrace his situation, warts and all. He learns that life isn't just about what you get out of it but how others benefit from the gestures and sacrifices of a life well lived.

Nobody had to teach that lesson to Jesus Christ; He embodies the lesson. The King of Kings was born in a humble manger filled with scratchy, smelly manger straw. His self-proclaimed purpose in Matthew 20:28 was "not to come to be served, but to serve, and to give His life as a ransom for many."

If you're an American consumer, you live in an era where companies market to your every need and desire, in a round-the-clock hope they will seduce you into buying their products. With the snap of a finger, we can enjoy the boldest and hottest coffee. Machines wash our dishes, cook our food, mow our manicured lawns, and launder our dirty clothes. We enjoy personal rights and freedoms unmatched in the world. Let's face it: sometimes we are put out by small sacrifices like taking out the garbage or picking up the animal waste in the yard.

It's probably impossible for us to imagine the voluntary

sacrifice that began for Jesus from the moment He was born. Though we don't know when in His young life He was actually cognizant of that sacrifice, He does tell His parents in Luke 2:49 at the age of twelve that He must "be about my father's business." As a boy, He embraced His purpose and fulfilled His destiny with courage, dignity, and self-control. Though He was tempted by Satan to thwart those plans in the desert, He continued His journey, even amidst the taunts of the priests and elders who mocked Him, shouting, "He saves others yet He cannot save Himself" (Matthew 27:42). He completed the grueling work on the cross.

What cross are you meant to endure and even embrace? Most of us would prefer not to even identify it or speak of it aloud. But God knows what it is—and you do, too. Jesus modeled the ultimate endurance so we can take up our own cross each day to live the life He redeemed for us with obedience and courage.

Keys to Kingdom Living: Give thanks to Jesus for embracing the cross!

Doorpost: "He himself bore our sins in His body on the tree, that we might die to sin and live to righteousness. By His wounds you have been healed." 1 Peter 2:24 (ESV)

THE CROSS: WHAT JESUS BORE

*T*he agony Jesus endured on the cross was both emotional and physical. Emotionally, we know that He was abandoned by most of the disciples, and those in the crowds who once followed Him had turned on Him, calling out to Pontius Pilate for His crucifixion. Also, in His first words on the cross, He speaks of feeling forsaken by God His Father.

But what unimaginable level of physical suffering did He endure? A doctor by the name of David Teresake wrote an article about the medical aspect of the crucifixion. He began it by pointing out that Jesus was forced to walk 2.5 miles following a sleepless, anguished night. As we read in Luke 22, Jesus prayed in the Garden of Gethesemane. Luke records that Jesus actually sweat drops of blood, a medical condition called hematidrosis that is caused by extreme stress and trauma.

The article goes on to describe the physical trauma of the flogging. Though the number of strikes is not recorded in the Bible, Jewish law stipulated initially the number was 40, but it was later reduced to 39. The whip used for such a punishment would typically feature bone and metal shards attached to the leather straps. Many victims of such a beating would die or at least be rendered unconscious, simply from the beating. Severe blood loss always resulted, as did a shredding of muscle mass and bone exposure from skin stripped from the back. The article mentions that the crown of thorns may have covered the entire scalp, and the thorns have been 1–2 inches long. Jesus also endured blows that drove the thorns deep into His head, causing severe bleeding.

It also mentions that, based on what is written in Isaiah 50:8, the Romans may have pulled His beard out. It also describes the 80 to 110 pounds of wood—the cross itself—that He had to carry at least part of the estimated 650 yards to Golgotha. We can infer from Scripture that Jesus fell with the cross while walking down the steps of the Antonio Fortress. Such a fall may have led, it points out, to a contusion of the heart, causing it to rupture once Jesus hung on the cross. The trauma caused by the 7-inch long and 3/8-inch wide nails punctured the median nerve in His wrists, causing shocks of pain to radiate in His arms. The article points out He would have been severely dehydrated, with loss of strength and severely restricted blood flow due to fluid in the lungs and their slowly collapsing state. All of these conditions led to a fatal strain on the heart and its inability to pump blood through the body.

Though Jesus's mortal heart may have failed in that moment, His heart for you and me did—and still does!—triumph over the grave as He willingly was led like a lamb to the slaughter" (Isaiah 53:7). No beating heart ever had a more noble demise.

Keys to Kingdom Living: Never take the cross and all accomplished on it for granted.

Doorpost: "[Let us fix] our eyes on Jesus, the author and perfecter of faith, who for the joy set before Him endured the cross, despising the shame, and has sat down at the right hand of the throne of God." Hebrews 12:2 (NASB)

THE CROSS: SYMBOLS AND
SIGNIFICANCE

*C*rosses in fashion and design remain iconic. They serve as reminders to Christians of the sacrificial life and death of Jesus, but not everyone who wears one gives its backstory the reverent attention it deserves. Cross symbols actually preceded the crucifixion and were popular symbols in ancient Egyptian and Hindu cultures. The actual wearing of crosses by Christians as symbols of their devotion to their Lord didn't come into practice until about the third century during the rule of Constantine. Today's crosses are worn both with—and, sadly, without—intention to convey a higher meaning.

In Acts 5, 10, and 13, the cross is described as a tree, using the original Greek word *xulon*. Trees are often written about in Scripture. The tree of the knowledge of good and evil, rife with forbidden fruit, proved to be the downfall of Adam and Eve. This rebellious act of eating symbolized Man acting apart from God, seeking knowledge not directly given by God and, in fact, opposing His will.

Tree branches are also discussed in Ezekiel, Jeremiah, and Zechariah; all contain reference to the Branch. And in Isaiah, chapter 11, we read, "And there shall come forth a rod out of the stem of Jesse, and a Branch shall grow out of its roots." Today we know and believe Jesus Christ, our Messiah, is that root.

Jesus spoke of the significance of vines and branches themselves, both living and pruned. In John 15:1, Jesus refers to himself as the True Vine and to His Father God as the Gardener. In John 15:6, Jesus says, "If anyone does not abide in me, he is thrown away like a branch and withers. And the branches are gathered, thrown into the fire and burned."

Ironically, while hanging on the cross Himself, a hyssop branch laced with sour wine was extended to Jesus for him to moisten His dry mouth. The Branch of Jesse refused this, instead taking on the full brunt of the torture on the cross to pay for our sins so our pruned branches could be grafted into His root. Because of this selfless act on the cross, we "branches" don't need to wither and die off the vine.

Jesus earned our redemption on the cross. We can abide in His root. In Romans 11, the branches represent the inclusion of Gentiles. We read, "And you, although a wild olive shoot, were grafted in among the others and now share in the nourishing root of the olive tree." The cross continues to remind us we are redeemed and immoveable.

Keys to Kingdom Living: As a follower of Christ, meditate on and truly ponder the meaning of the cross each time you see one, and thank your Savior for all He's done.

Doorpost: "Blessed is the one who trusts in the Lord, whose confidence is in Him. They will be like a tree planted by the water that sends out its roots by the stream. It does not fear when heat comes; its leaves are always green. It has no worries in a year of drought and never fails to bear fruit." Jeremiah 17:7–8

THE CROSS: WHERE WE LEAVE
OUR SINS

I have a confession to make. I have BPS, otherwise known as Big Purse Syndrome. I am compelled to carry everything around in my big purse where runaway breath mints and scraps of paper keep company with important receipts and a sea of loose credit and ID cards. Far more organized friends chastise me with humor and well-intentioned advice regarding the dangers of BPS and the potential remedies.

I do try to seize spare moments to clean out the clutter. Sometimes, I even make sure my "presidents" face the same way in my wallet, like my accounting friend does. Sometimes if I'm in a real hurry, I will just change purses, leaving behind the clutter to deal with another time. One more skeleton outta my closet!

If we are honest with ourselves, most of us suffer to some degree from BPS when it comes to cleaning out our sin clutter and disposing of it. We might be faithful to begin the process, confessing our sins to God. But when it comes to our personal inventory of wrongdoing, our self-imposed ranking systems deem some sins more "unforgiveable" than others. The Enemy might get a foothold and try to convince us that something we've done is too big for God to forgive. When a notion like this is allowed to fester, it blocks fellowship with God. It also prevents true absolution, because it's bestowed but unaccepted. It may, in some cases, even result in a person turning from God because of the mistaken belief that he or she is unworthy.

We are told in Revelation 5:2 that only "the Lion of the tribe of Judah, the Root of David . . . is able to open the scroll and its seven seals." Because He triumphed over sin and death, fulfilled the law, and paid the price for us, only He is worthy. He extends forgiveness and grace for us because our debt was paid on the cross. We can't earn or deserve this free gift; we only need to repent of what we've done wrong and embrace what Jesus has already done to right your wrongs.

Paul is a poster child for nailing his past misdeeds to the cross. Before his conversion, he persecuted and murdered early Christians. So when he wrote in 2 Corinthians 5:17 about how thoroughly God wipes our slate clean, nobody knew better than he did what that forgiveness truly feels and looks like. "Therefore, if anyone is in Christ, he is a new creation. The old has passed away, the new has come."

We can't fall victim to BPS and leave our clutter behind. We have to guard against putting our new wine into old wineskins, as Jesus warns in Luke 5:37. We need to constantly renew ourselves inside and out by sincerely repenting and continually accepting God's grace in all its fullness so we can be what God intended every day.

Keys to Kingdom Living: Ask for, and receive, forgiveness without attaching strings.

Doorpost: "If we confess our sins, He is faithful and just and will forgive us our sins and purify us from all unrighteousness." 1 John 1:9

THE CROSS: THE THORN WE BEAR
WITH GRACE

*H*ow many times have we talked about "the cross we have to bear"? We may flippantly toss these words out over something insignificant, in an almost joking way, about some obligation that is more of an annoyance than a true sacrifice.

In fact, the crosses we bear are sometimes so abhorrent to us that we are barely able to bring ourselves to acknowledge or discuss them. Paul did not mention his cross by name. He called it a "thorn in his side" in 2 Corinthians 12:7. One cross I bear is the emotional and physical strain of my younger son's autism. Even this morning as I was preparing to work on this devotion, my sixteen-year-old son autistic son wet the bed. His linens, just changed the day before, needed to be washed and replaced once his mattress was dry.

I must confess I do not always accomplish these kinds of tasks as if I were "working for God and not men," as we are told to do in Colossians 3:23. My selfish nature takes over and my sense of entitlement kicks into high gear. Why does the daily care of my teenager look more like the care of a two year old? How long will I need to commit to it? How can I possibly bear the load and responsibility "as unto the Lord"?

The truth is, I can't. It's the kind of undertaking that is God-sized, and therefore must be God-shouldered. He tells us to come to Him when we are weary and He will give us rest, that His "yoke is easy" and the "burden is light." God doesn't mean for us to carry such heavy loads alone. He wants us to depend on Him and ask Him to help us carry it.

Do I manage to share my burden 100 percent of the time? Of course not. In fact, I can't. I try to play Hot Potato with my burden. I toss it to God when it's too hot to touch. Somehow I grab it back again and then toss it back to Him when my fingers burn. Fortunately, He never tosses it back to me. Instead, He wants to continually shoulder it. In the famous hymn, "What a Friend We Have in Jesus," the words found there both comfort and convict. "Oh what peace we often forfeit/Oh what needless pain we bear/All because we do not carry/Everything to God in prayer."

I must continually repent of selfishness, ask God to give me a sacrificial heart, and do whatever it takes to care for my son as long as I am able—with God's help and the heart attitude of Jesus. I temper this commitment with a prayer for discernment as to how and when God's plans for my youngest son's life will change. What I do know is that I must remain focused on God's will for my life and for my sons, so that when and if the day comes for this burden to be lifted, it will be out of obedience to Him.

Keys to Kingdom Living: When we endure burdens, with God's help, we die to self as Jesus did.

Doorpost: "Present your bodies as a living sacrifice, holy and acceptable to God." Romans 12:1 (ESV)

THE CROSS: MODELING AND TEACHING OTHERS HOW THE THORN IS BORNE

*M*y autistic son Max might be nonverbal and unable to follow most spoken instructions, but he is a very keen observer. This skill has served him well in helping him accomplish his somewhat limited goals. For instance, he has memorized a four-digit password and learned how to enter it into his iPad. He is then able to select the YouTube app from the screen filled with several apps, choose from yet another field of twenty or so video icons, and then identify and play the film clip of his choice via streaming. This might not sound like much of an achievement, but for Max it's huge.

Max is not alone in learning more from watching than from words. If someone provides advice, we are less likely to trust their information if we have seen them do something in their own life that that runs counter to the values and beliefs we embrace.

The same holds true for those we parent, mentor, or hope to bring into the fold. If we constantly complain about our lives, are we behaving as God's ambassadors? Is our glass always half empty, our day always terrible, our lot in life always more than we can bear? If those are the things coming out of our mouths in front of our children, how can we expect them to be attracted to the faith? They are watching us carefully and care more about what we're doing than what we're saying.

Back when my oldest son was in kindergarten, he asked me what Jesus did with his quarters (his Sunday school offering). It struck me in that moment that he didn't understand the connection between giving and its end result. I went to the principal of the church school and told her God gave me an idea for the Loaves and Fishes program. Each month a different global, national, or local need would be addressed. We would educate the kids about the need and explain whenever possible the impact the offerings would have.

The principal agreed to implement it and I began making plans to run it. Shortly after, a series of events transpired causing the church administrators to tell me we were no longer permitted to bring our younger son Max to the children's program on Sunday. We were crushed; we needed to find a new church. Though I didn't move my older son from the school, the rejection of my youngest child was a bitter pill to swallow. I prayed about what to do and pleaded with the Lord to allow me to step down from Loaves and Fishes. But He was adamant: do the work I have called you to do, period. My oldest son watched me swallow my pride as God enabled me to do the work with joy—and it had an impact on all who knew what had happened to me. We have to model servitude to God no matter the price.

Keys to Kingdom Living: Teach others to bear their cross by faithfully bearing your own.

Doorpost: "Whoever claims to live in Him must live as Jesus did." 1 John 2:6

THE CROSS: X MARKS THE SPOT

*T*here comes a point when everyone reaches a crossroad in life about what kind of belief system they're going to embrace, what will determine the direction of their course, and how they intend to move forward once those choices are made. Even though everyone reaches this point, not everyone recognizes they are there, so they may not have a clue about how to proceed once they reach this crossroad. Some people, in their confusion, take a detour instead, going down a road they think will mark self-discovery, only to discover it is riddled with potholes and blind, self-destructive turns.

It may not seem like it when we stand at that fork in the road, but each choice we make has the potential for hidden consequences. While in college, I vacationed in Mexico with friends. We went to dinner and were walking back to the hotel when I saw a ferry that was boarding to go out to a cruise ship. I hatched a plan for us to jump on the ferry, board the ship, mingle, and return later to shore. (I had never been on a cruise and knew nothing about the protocol.)

I managed to convince my friends to get on board, but one by one, they thought it over and disembarked. Standing alone, I too got off the ferry. The next morning, I looked out the window and saw that the ship had a hammer and a sickle: it was a Russian cruise ship featuring a Communist symbol concealed by the darkness! Though the idea of being afraid seems a little silly now, I remember thinking back then not to ever consider jumping into something before I had carefully weighed all aspects.

When we are presented with the Good News of Jesus Christ, we stand at that crossroad. We can choose to follow Jesus or walk away from Him. God didn't create robots pre-programmed to obey Him; He's looking for authentic followers. The Lord invites everyone to His table, but not all invitees will be seated for the banquet. In Matthew 22:8–14, we read of the invited guests who tried to come to the wedding feast improperly clothed and as a result were cast out from the festivities. "For many are called but few are chosen" sums up the two-way street of salvation recorded in verse 14: God does the inviting, but man must RSVP before the Holy Spirit dwells. We must deliberately choose Christ.

Have you RSVP'd to Jesus's calling? Or are you carting around the invite as if you have all the time in the world to reply? Have you accepted and expressed gratitude for being included? Anyone still holding onto the card is at the crossroad. Time is too precious to waste.

Keys to Kingdom Living: Say yes to Jesus and turn the corner on your life journey today.

Doorpost: "Behold, I stand at the door and knock. If anyone hears my voice and opens the door, I will come in to him and eat with him, and he with me." Revelation 3:20 (ESV)

WEEK 9: UNWRAPPING PRESENT MOMENT GIFTS

UNWRAPPING PRESENT MOMENT GIFTS: THE DIVINE EXAMPLE

On hearing the expression "every day is a present," you may find yourself holding an unwrapped box in hand, eager to regift it. If we are honest, we have all had those regiftable days. There's nothing like a lofty platitude to bring out the cynic in you.

There is a funny scene from the film *Tootsie* where Dustin Hoffman, playing an out-of-work actor who is down on his luck, sees a mime performing his act in the park. As the mime atop a curb dramatically teeters on his "tightrope," Hoffman reaches out and knocks the mime down to the grassy ground.

You probably haven't decked a mime. But don't we sometimes roll our eyes at the perpetually upbeat mime in the middle of a bad day? Rather than identifying what is good in our day, we wallow in the bad, and sometimes even try to drag others down with us. This kind of thinking, if left unchecked, eats away at the soul—and before you know it, you are on your way to becoming a grouch of epic proportions.

Perhaps you've heard the saying, "What if you woke up tomorrow with only what you were thankful for yesterday?" Being grateful to God for what we have is a good starting point for any day. But framing a good attitude each day also involves developing an overcoming attitude for any visible obstacles and embracing the unknown as you navigate through it.

As I worked on this book, I was frustrated about how much more time it was taking me to complete it than I'd initially envisioned. I was behind schedule. I called my mentor earlier in the day and left a message. As I was driving myself to a dinner party that night, she returned my call. She was at JFK on her way to Israel, so I pulled over for a moment to talk to her. She had talked to God before calling me back. She dispensed golden nuggets of advice: "God is more concerned with His input than your output." Whoa! As we continued talking, I began to drive around aimlessly in the vicinity of the party but without a clue as to where I was going. As our conversation came to a close, I managed to arrive at my destination at the proper time. It was on God's timetable and with His "nav"!

Jesus always arrived at His destination at the proper time, even when His friends didn't share His timetable. When He arrived after Lazarus died—rather than before—Mary and Martha were confused (John 11). And when He arrived at Jairus's home after his daughter had passed, that timetable was questioned (Luke 8:41). But He raised both of them from the dead. Any earlier and the miracles would have been missed.

Keys to Kingdom Living: Are you going through the motions and missing miracles, or looking to God for guidance?

Doorpost: "God is our refuge and strength, a very present help in trouble." Psalm 46:1 (ESV)

UNWRAPPING PRESENT MOMENT
GIFTS: ELEVATING THE PAST

*T*hinking of the past with any real perspective is almost impossible. People either romanticize it all out of proportion or let what was tragic or painful drag them down like an albatross.

As with everything in life, balance is critical when evaluating our past. Healthy attitudes are tricky. The good old days had their share of problems too. I remember when my husband was in law school and we were living off of our savings and my small salary. If I were to romanticize, I might say we lived on love, since we were young and strong and beautifully poised to enjoy successful careers. But someone inclined to dwell on the negative might instead recall how we were burglarized twice, pickpocketed, carjacked, embroiled in a fraud scheme at a crummy job I took, and were victims of a terrible car accident. Depending on the evaluation, a romantic or pessimistic case could be made for the same three-year time frame.

Jesus didn't long for yesterday. Each day when He set out to minister to others, He focused on the events happening in the moment. He didn't fret not having gone to the store to get bread before a crowd gathered, but instead assembled available food, blessed it, and fed 5,000 people at a moment's notice. When He was anguished in the garden before His inevitable crucifixion, He wasn't waxing nostalgic over His boyhood days helping

Joseph in the woodshop. He was focused on the business at hand, authentically talking to His Father and praying to Him.

We don't do ourselves any favors longing for the past, trying to recreate it, or remaining emotionally stuck in our thought life. A great example of this kind of warped thinking occurs in Exodus 16:3 when the Israelites recall their time in Egypt. Instead of recalling their enslavement and thanking God for their release, they spoke of an alternate reality, saying, "If only we had died by the Lord's hand in Egypt! There we sat around pots of meat and ate all the food we wanted . . ." No mention was made of the long hours of work and the lack of freedom they enjoyed serving their Egyptian masters.

Romanticizing the past only serves to frustrate and stagnate our future endeavors. It is a trick of the Enemy to undermine our effectiveness for God in moving forward. It also undermines our trust in God's plan for our lives.

When my hubby and I began looking for our first house (when it became painfully apparent we couldn't yet afford a home), I began moping and slipped into a funk. Years later, when God paved the way for a miraculous real estate deal, I could see how God's plan unfolded for our lives. By staying in the moment, we stay the course, do God's bidding day to day, and are poised to see what He will do tomorrow.

Keys to Kingdom Living: Hold thoughts of the past captive and be ready for tomorrow.

Doorpost: "Do not call to mind the former things, or ponder things of the past." Isaiah 43:18 (NASB)

UNWRAPPING PRESENT MOMENT
GIFTS: LETTING GO OF THE PAST

*S*ometimes tragic events or poor choices we have made
will drag us down in the present to such a degree that
we can't move forward emotionally or physically. Though the
circumstances of these different scenarios certainly vary, the
outcome can be the same. The mother whose son was killed by
a drunk driver may relive the moment over and over again for
decades and never recover from the pain of this unimaginable
tragedy. Or the guilt of a teenage drunk driver might destroy his
ability to move forward with his own life, feeling he doesn't
deserve a future because of what he has done.

As Christians, we know we can face the truth about
ourselves, repent, and be "cleansed from all unrighteousness," as
Scripture states in 1 John 1:9. But when we drag around our
guilt and shame, we're not honoring God. We are, in fact,
denying He is the Messiah who took away the sins of the world.
God does not want His people to sit with their pain or their
shame; He wants them to move on without reliving their
mistakes. That is not to say there will not be consequences to
mistakes, but living with consequences is far different than being
frozen with them and the choice from which they sprung.

When David repented for arranging for Uriah to be killed in
battle in order to marry Bathsheba who was pregnant with his
son, he didn't sit in his shame even though he endured the death

of their son as a consequence of his wrongdoing. Though David could have withdrawn from everyone and even possibly turned away from God, he instead chose to accept God's grace. As a result, we are the fortunate readers of many of the most beautiful, authentic writings in the Bible about God's redemptive mercy.

When I visited Rwanda on a mission trip in the early 2000s, I learned invaluable lessons about forgiveness and redemption. One Sunday a man stood up in front of the church and talked about how, during the genocide in the '90s, he had murdered the tribesmen with whom longstanding war had been waged. He then spoke of a relative of a man whose family members he had murdered. He told the amazing story of how that man not only forgave him but took him into his house and loved him like a family member. It was hard for me to imagine being capable of that level of forgiveness. The man himself said he did not forgive alone, but with God's help. Because both of them let go of the past, each had the ability to be restored.

If you are holding onto a poor choice from the past, release it and accept redemption once and for all. If pain from the past is dragging you down, lay out your sorrow before God and ask Him to help heal you so you can move forward.

Keys to Kingdom Living: Put the past behind you and step forward, letting His light guide you each day, one step at a time.

Doorpost: "[Forget] what lies behind and [reach] forward to what lies ahead." Philippians 3:13 (NASB)

UNWRAPPING PRESENT MOMENT GIFTS: WELCOMING DIVINE APPOINTMENTS

*Y*ou may have heard of the term "divine appointment" in reference to how God leads us unexpectedly to someplace and then to someone who either needs our help or offers help to us. Many of us have been on the giving or receiving end of this powerful experience.

People who know me well know the only thing I hate more than driving is filling my car up with gas. As a result, I've been known to ignore the fuel gauge in my car on more than one occasion. One day I was on my way to Bible study and had forgotten about the low fuel warning the previous day until I got into the car. Inexplicably, I decided not to take the freeway. Convinced I could make it on time with the fuel I had, I pressed on—only to run out of gas in the middle of the street. Providentially, I was a few yards from a gas station. In the middle of the intersection, trying to figure out what to do next, three men came alongside the car and began pushing, telling me to put the car into neutral gear. As I turned into the gas station, I felt thankful from head to toe that my vehicle and I were now positioned for rescue. When I turned to thank the men, they had literally disappeared. Angels or good Samaritans, who's to say?

I was dramatically rescued in that divine appointment. But the divine appointments that inconvenience us, where we are the ones doing the helping, often don't happen because we don't welcome the interruption and might even avoid it altogether. When Jesus was on His way to Galilee, He encountered the Samaritan woman at the well. He was keeping a divine appointment even though His chosen route to Samaria was not the established route for the Jews, who felt it was beneath them to travel though an area where the despised people dwelled. Jesus entered the "side door" to Samaria to keep the divine appointment at the well. Our Good Shepherd will leave the 99 sheep to go after the one that was lost, as we are told in Luke 15:4. But will we? Are we willing to stray from the path of the day to help someone in need, or do we take the more established route?

As I was writing this, I stopped to accept a delivery at the front door. I saw a painter in front of my neighbor's house who handles little projects for me from time to time. He'd gotten a new phone and I'd been trying to find him. When I saw him, I went over to tell him to call me about a future job, thinking I would get right back to my work. But he wanted to come in and immediately get things going, so I relented and he came inside. He then shared that he had no work and that he needed the money. I told him it was a miracle from God that I saw him and he agreed. I then told two other people about him, and within the hour he had work from them as well. We all rejoiced! God's timetable is better than ours; to God be the glory!

Keys to Kingdom Living: Welcome and rejoice in your divine appointments, giving thanks to the serendipitous way God uses you as well as blesses you.

Doorpost: "In all your ways acknowledge Him, and He will make straight your paths." Proverbs 3:6 (ESV)

UNWRAPPING PRESENT MOMENT
GIFTS: EMBRACING EACH DAY'S JOY

*W*e've all seen and heard the verse, "This is the day that the Lord has made, let us rejoice and be glad in it," from Psalm 118:24. I believe in the transforming power of this verse, and I actually have a custom stencil of it in my walk-in closet over the window. Every morning, when I'm dressing in my closet, I have the opportunity to read this verse, meditate on its truths, choose to thank God, and embrace the joy that can be found in it every day as I live in relationship with Him. Sometimes the sun shines brightly through the window. Recently a friend was lifting me up in prayer and asked that I would be able to feel God's love shine on my back like the warm sun. I think of this now as I get ready in the morning and thank God for the day.

By now you may be rolling your eyes. You might be thinking I'm throwing out platitudes and not being honest about what daily life on the planet Earth is really like. And you would be right. Because even though that option is available to us all every day, I don't always choose that joy. Some days I wake up and if I don't "take every thought captive," as is suggested in 2 Corinthians 10:5, my glass is half empty before I fill up my coffee mug.

To be fair, this task is easier on some days than others. I remember taking great comfort on hearing an excellent sermon on this topic. The speaker pointed out a truth about this verse often overlooked. It does not say we have to rejoice "about" the day. Thankfully, we aren't commanded to thank God for the flat tire we had this morning, our husband's layoff, or our prodigal child's drug problem. Instead, the verse welcomes us to take comfort in the reminder that God has a plan and purpose for every day. When morning arrives, we can be thankful for the promise of the day itself. Yesterday's worries need not be remembered, and the concerns of tomorrow can wait until then. Truly, we can always find something to be thankful for.

I learned some valuable lessons connected to this verse on my mission trip to Rwanda. Most of the people in the remote village were barefoot. They lived in simple mud huts with no-frills homemade beds on the floor and simple wooden benches for seating. Their artwork on the walls consisted primarily of newspaper clippings crudely applied to the surface. Few of the homes had electricity, and none had indoor plumbing. Few had cars, motorcycles, or even bicycles. Most had to walk miles for their water and carry it in containers back to their dwellings.

Despite a lack of creature comforts, the people we encountered inside the church on the hill were filled to the brim with the joy of the Lord. Though many had lost family members and loved ones in the genocide of the '90s that killed an estimated one million people, they enthusiastically sang praise songs about heaven and their love for God. They didn't gloss over their pain or inconvenience—but they didn't dwell on it, either. Instead, they overcame adversity by celebrating each day's joy.

Keys to Kingdom Living: Find joy in every day the Lord gives you and be glad in that day.

Doorpost: "Rejoice always, pray continually, give thanks in all circumstances; for this is God's will for you in Christ Jesus." 1 Thessalonians 5:16

UNWRAPPING PRESENT MOMENT GIFTS: SAYING NO TO TOMORROW'S WORRY

I know a woman who is paralyzed by the possibilities of the future, both short- and long-term. She refuses to swim in the ocean. She is consumed by thoughts of potential natural disasters. She white-knuckles the wheel when she's driving and micromanages others as they drive. For her, illness is around every corner. As a friend, I remind her that worry might actually shorten her life. Yet, she simply shrugs her shoulders, says it's how she is wired and can't help it.

But the truth is that we can—with God's help. He invites us to give it all to Him in Matthew 11:29, when He says His "burden is light." God does not mean for us to stay awake at night worrying about the next president or whether nuclear war is imminent. While concern—and subsequent prayer—about the issues of the day is appropriate, the counterproductive state of worry is not. In fact, worry is the antithesis of trust in God and therefore it is both a sin and barrier to intimate relationship with Him.

We can begin the process of freeing ourselves from worry about tomorrow by identifying the difference between concern and worry. That difference lies more in approach than actual definitions. A little light bulb went on in my head when I read this on a job coaching website: "Worry is problem oriented.

Concern is solution oriented." We can't resolve all concerns but we can manage them.

Worry registers higher on the Richter scale of emotional seismic activity than concern does. A concerned person may weigh potential solutions, taking a more logical approach to handling them by putting pen to paper. They recognize and accept what may not change. Worriers let things spin around in their heads. They don't take irrational thoughts captive. They don't permit perspective or seek wise counsel; instead, they're inclined to vent or isolate themselves as their blood pressure steadily rises.

I believe there was a reason Jesus gave the famous Sermon on the Mount. When you're on top of a mountain, you have perspective over all that is below you, but when you stand on a flat plain, you don't have a complete view. A worrier sees the plain, but the concerned Christian takes a mountaintop viewpoint, as Jesus did in Matthew 6:27 when He says, "Can any one of you by worrying add a single hour to your life?" He never worried, but instead moved forward in faith as He marched to the cross.

Thankfully, both the concerned and the worried are invited to ditch their burdens. "Cast your cares on the Lord and He will sustain you; He will never let the righteous be shaken" (Psalm 55:22). When you do, and you stand on the mountaintop of God's perspective, you are securely positioned to endure.

Keys to Kingdom Living: Give God your burdens and just say "no" to the trap of worry.

Doorpost: "Therefore do not worry about tomorrow, for tomorrow will worry about itself. Each day has enough trouble of its own." Matthew 6:34

UNWRAPPING PRESENT MOMENT GIFTS: TRUSTING IN JOY FOR THE FINAL TOMORROW

*I*f you have ever been in the presence of a strong Christian who was completely ready to meet their Maker, you don't soon forget their amazing level of peace. I had the pleasure and privilege of being with a handful of such people as they prepared to claim their glorious inheritance.

One, in particular, embodied what it means to fully trust in the ultimate tomorrow. As a young orphan placed in a Christian home in her native Philippines, she had devoted herself to the Lord at an early age. Throughout her life as an unmarried woman who suffered from many health challenges, she chose joy and filled her life with worship and service to her Father God. Her choices could have been much different. She could have spent her life complaining about being lonely, about her aches and pains and serious illness, and even about the financial struggles she endured. Yet she faced battle after battle with cancer, endured kidney dialysis, and finally complications from a stroke with courage and conviction, knowing in her mind and heart exactly where she was going.

She would testify to these truths in her hospice bed to anyone who would listen for as long as she was still able to speak. On one of the last nights of her life, I stopped by her room to visit and could see she was no longer able to converse. I talked to her awhile and eventually decided to play "Revelation Song" by Phillips, Craig & Dean from my phone music library. As I held her hand and sang along with the artists in the room, her lips began to move. I could see her body becoming animated during the song. Slowly, deliberately, she began to raise her only good hand in the air, as high as she could, praising Him in the only way her body was still able but clearly with 100 percent of her heart and mind.

I will never forget this moment, and I was honored God let me be a part of it. Seeing her valiant overcoming attitude helped model for me how I want to spend my last days, if I have the ability to plan. If I am able in those days, I want to praise God for all He did in my life, thank Him for however many days He gave me, and model for others what that trust can look like as we look forward to eternity in paradise with the King of Kings and Lord of Lords.

We don't need to wait until we are dying to imagine the joy we will experience in the New Jerusalem. In John 17:16, Jesus said that we "are not of the world, even as I am not of it." When we live with the perspective that we are checked into a motel while we wait to settle into kingdom digs, we can endure hardship with a Christian perspective. Our "momentary troubles are achieving for us an eternal glory," as Paul said in 2 Corinthians 4:17. Checkout time is coming.

Keys to Kingdom Living: Live in faith today as you anticipate tomorrow's joy.

Doorpost: "But our citizenship is in heaven, and from it we await a Savior, the Lord Jesus Christ, who will transform our lowly body to be like His glorious body, by the power that enables Him even to subject all things to Himself." Philippians 3:20–21 (ESV)

WEEK 10: LOVE

LOVE: BIRTHING THE ULTIMATE GIFT
AND SACRIFICE

*T*he John 3:16 Bible verse is widely memorized and quoted. But how often do we really unpack and ponder the deep meaning it conveys, or meditate on the life-changing truths found within it?

The radical notion that any father would sacrifice the life of his son for anyone is unimaginable. As loving, caring parents, it is nearly impossible to envision anything or anyone coming before the welfare of our offspring. Most of us would lay down our lives for our children.

But God really did "so love the world" that this is exactly what He did. Out of His great love He crafted a plan that demanded great personal cost. And Jesus, who sacrificed Himself "as a ransom for many" (Matt. 20:28), laid down His own life to accomplish the work He was born to undertake.

I can't speak for you, but I know in my own life there are moments when I feel rejected, despised, ostracized, marginalized, and dehumanized. It is in those moments when I need God's love the most that I don't immediately feel His deep love. I have made it a goal to try to be deeply mindful of God's love in these dark passages. I keep Bible verses about His love nearby so I can refer to them and be reminded of it. When we are able to wrap His perfect love and His trustworthy promises around us, they serve as a shield against the slings and arrows the

Enemy hurls as he tries to take us down daily. We are told in 1 John 4:9 that "the love of God was made manifest among us, that God sent His only Son into the world, so that we might live through Him" (ESV).

When we are truly able to live through Jesus, our hearts are filled with a sacrificial love for others and we too become more like Christ. People like Corrie ten Boom, Mother Teresa, Jim Elliot, and a host of other missionaries and servants of God devoted their lives to the work of spreading God's love to a hurting world.

When Jesus issued the Great Commission to His disciples in Matthew 28, He wasn't only commanding them to use words to spread the gospel with their lips and tongues. He was sending them out as His ambassadors of love. Jesus knew that the walk was even more important than the talk. Are we genuinely loving ambassadors of Christ? Are we willing and ready to sacrifice whatever it takes so we can bring more people to Him?

Keys to Kingdom Living: Truly thank God for the love gift of His Son, your Savior.

Doorpost: "For to us a child is born, to us a son is given, and the government will be on His shoulders. And He will be called Wonderful Counselor, Mighty God, Everlasting Father, Prince of Peace." Isaiah 9:6

LOVE: THAT PROMPTED REDEMPTION

I've had to come to terms with a terrible truth about myself as I've become older: I am a grudge holder. When someone does something unkind or unjust, even unconsciously, I internalize it on a deep and personal level. Then, as if that weren't crazy enough, I add a cherry on the top by blowing it all out of proportion.

Though I have been doing this for much of my life, I only recently became aware of it on a conscious level. A friend gave me some psychological worksheets designed to help uncover the roots of deep-seated issues. In a nutshell, they probe your thoughts on a situation, ask for God's truth about it, ask you to restate a positive truth that negates your misconception regarding your own perception, and finally has you state what could be learned moving forward.

Every time I complete these worksheets, a common thread appears: my inability to forgive and dispense grace to those I love without keeping a record of wrongs. If we love at the highest level, we are called to forgive as we have been forgiven. God doesn't keep a record of wrongs. He promises sinners in Hebrews 8:12 that He will "be merciful to their unrighteousness, and their sins and their iniquities will I remember no more." He tells us that He does it not only for us—He also does it for Himself as we learn in Isaiah 43:24–25. "You have burdened me with your sins; you have wearied me with your iniquities. I, even I, am He who blots out your transgressions for my own sake, and I will not remember your sins." Our sins are "cast into the depths of the sea" (Micah 7:19), "put behind His back" (Isaiah 44:22), and "covered with a thick cloud" (Isaiah 44:22). God doesn't want, or need, to be burdened with our sin. His divine plan settled the score more than 2,000 years ago. Jesus paid the price when He died on the cross to redeem the whole world. We pay a twofold price when we don't forgive those who have wronged us. We retain the burden of experiencing wrongs done to us. We aren't built to walk around with feelings of pent-up anger or resentment. We are told in Mark 11:25 that if are praying and we have a grievance against anyone, we are to immediately let it go and forgive them. If we continue to harbor resentment, we crowd out love and forgiveness. When we choose forgiveness, we are able to release the negative feelings associated with that uncomfortable state and enter into a state of true love, boundless freedom, and amazing grace. When we dispense grace, we can also experience freedom.

If we don't forgive, we pay yet another price. We learn a hard truth in Matthew 6:15 that "if you do not forgive others their sins, neither will our Father forgive yours." As children of God, we need to be gracious enough to forgive and humble enough to recognize its importance, rejoicing that we, too, are forgiven.

Keys to Kingdom Living: Love means we are forgiven and must also freely forgive.

Doorpost: "As far as the east is from the west, so far has He removed our transgressions from us." Psalm 103:12

LOVE: BLESSED BY GOD BETWEEN MEN AND WOMEN

*T*he delicate dance of love between a man and a woman ebbs and flows with harmony and discord. It is fraught with missteps as much as it is beautified by a unique harmony when a couple's movements flow with beautiful synchronicity. Regardless of the state of the dance at any given time, God knew that Man was not meant to be alone, or to dance alone. Since the dawn of creation, God knew that human beings would never thrive in long-term isolation. God created women to accompany men on their journey and be helpmates to them.

You might feel like that term sounds somewhat demeaning —but, like so many other translations from the Hebrew found in the Bible, a closer look helps us understand what God meant. The literal translation from the Hebrew is "help meet." It is derived from the two words *ezer* and *k'enegedo*. *Ezer* in the Hebrew means "to rescue or save." The *k'enegedo* portion of the word means "to be strong." Author Diana Webb points out in her book *Forgotten Women of God* that *k'enegado* can also mean "against," which seems oddly ill-fitting in this case. However, on deeper study she learned that it meant "opposite of," as is the case with someone looking in a mirror and seeing another image closely resembling yourself that is, of course, a replica of your image. God, in fact, completed and delivered Adam by providing Eve, a helpmate with qualities he lacked. Eve also benefitted from the qualities Adam possessed that she did not have. I find that to be true in my own life.

I have been married for 35 years to a man my family used to describe as "the male me," though we are different in as many ways as we are similar. He is technical and likes to take charge. I'm artistic and literary and tend to go with the flow. Our household responsibilities are delineated according to what each does best. Though we don't always agree on everything, when it comes to core and fundamental values, we are almost always on the same page. Over the years we have learned a great deal about one another, about compromise, and about supporting each other in the ways that count. We have learned that in times of true adversity we can count on one another. And in the toughest times, under the most difficult circumstances, we have remembered that commitment trumps catastrophe. I really do believe that God orchestrated it all, because when I met my spouse I had no wisdom about how to choose a mate with solid, enduring qualities—and yet that is exactly what God gave me. Though my awareness of it in my youth was close to nil, today I often reflect on God's gift with deep thankfulness.

Of course, marriage has as many moments in the valley as it does on the mountaintop, and maybe even more. But God's design is one that we can be sure is intended to enhance our time here on earth as we learn how to love and work together in a spirit of cooperation, helpfulness, mutual respect, and sacrifice.

Keys to Kingdom Living: God blesses unions between man and woman.

Doorpost: "Therefore a man shall leave his father and his mother and hold fast to his wife, and they shall become one flesh." Genesis 1:24 (ESV)

LOVE: FOR OUR CHILDREN

*T*he first time I watched the 1994 remake of *Little Women*, I began sobbing uncontrollably within the first ten minutes. My husband and I had been trying to conceive a child for many years with no success. It didn't even occur to me that watching that movie would exacerbate my pangs for motherhood. The beautiful hot chocolate kind of moment, with the girls in their frilly nightgowns piled into bed with their mom, was enough to send me right over the edge and press the off button on the remote.

A generation later, blessed with a family built through adoption, I realize that hot chocolate moments are the tip of the parenting iceberg. Motherhood is filled with trips to the emergency room, disciplinary struggles, heartbreaking disappointments, and moments of self-doubt so excruciating I occasionally question whether or not I was meant to undertake the challenging experience at all. Fortunately, those low moments don't last long. Even though parenting a child with ADHD and another with severe autism hasn't been a walk in the park, I'm thankful to God for the two blessings He gave me and the opportunity to love and care for them.

Paternal love is more primal in nature than other kinds of love. Most mothers I know would lay down their very lives for their children—and, in fact, they do sacrifice themselves daily in a variety of ways for the best interests of their offspring. While some of that comes naturally, other forms of sacrifice are learned behaviors. I have been blessed in my life with some amazing godly mentors who came alongside in my parenting journey in prayer as well as in practical ways. They modeled firm yet gentle parenting. They provided tools, resources, and wisdom that still serve me today in my parenting, both under my roof and beyond as I try to extend my influence to my college son when he permits.

Part of remaining a good parent to adult children is providing a sounding board and a listening ear to their concerns with a reduced emphasis on solving or managing their daily affairs. I continue to be surprised at how, and when, my son seeks my input, and equally taken aback when I feel he needs my advice and doesn't seek it! It is in times like these that I remind myself of the love passages in 1 Corinthians 13. I tell myself that love for my sons "is patient and kind; love does not envy or boast; it is not arrogant or rude. It does not rejoice a wrongdoing, but rejoices with the truth. Love bears all things, hopes all things, endures all things. Love never ends."

I find that these passages are helpful in different ways in parenting my oldest who is maturing and my youngest who, in his disability, may always be a child. When we look to the Bible for words about loving our children, the pearls of wisdom we find there will enrich our inheritance to them as well as the inheritance they'll pass on.

Keys to Kingdom Living: Ideal parental love is best supported with godly wisdom.

Doorpost: "Do not provoke your children to anger, but bring them up in the discipline and instruction of the Lord." Ephesians 6:4 (NASB)

LOVE: FOR OUR FRIENDS

I remember being in junior high school and signing yearbooks with the acronym LYLAS. Translated, this tagline read Love Ya Like a Sister. The tagline was implemented with little discretion; after all, we were just goofy teenagers. The girlfriends I have in my life now whom I love like sisters mean far more to me than any LYLAS scribble could communicate.

After my son began to display his autistic behaviors, it became easy for me to see who my real friends were going to be. The revelations were truly surprising. The church we'd been attending for more than ten years suddenly did not welcome our family anymore. The invitations for dinner at other people's houses began to diminish. During a period in my life when I needed more help and more genuine love and concern, I found myself receiving less.

Fortunately, two important things happened in my life that changed its course and healed my isolation. The first was the introduction of new faith communities into my life. We joined a church with a growing ministry for developmentally disabled kids. Our son was welcomed and loved. As parents, we were supported by a life group of caring adults and friends. I became closely intertwined with an interdenominational Bible study where the women truly entered into my pain, encouraged me, and loved me in ways that bring me to tears even today as I write this.

The second way God delivered me from my isolation and retrieved me from my pity party is by introducing me to a book called *The Power of a Positive Friend*. Authors Karol Ladd and Terry Ann Kelly share practical principles on how to be a friend and truly nurture friendship on a deeply divine level. The wisdom it contained enabled me to enrich the friendships I already enjoyed and cultivate new and lasting ones while becoming the friend I wanted to have for myself. In reading this book, and working on my own friendship skills, I was able to "transform myself by the renewing" of my mind, as we read in Romans 12:2.

Over time, God answered my prayer, and in it He changed my heart and my attitude. Instead of moping around with a "woe is me" attitude, I began to invest in people who were already my friends in the deep and meaningful way I wanted them to invest in me. I also identified acquaintances I already knew and worked steadily with sincere effort to deepen those relationships with genuine affection and encouragement. Today, as a result of this book, my efforts, and God's answer to my prayer, I enjoy a cornucopia of meaningful relationships and consider myself blessed with many friends—and I believe I, too, am a blessing to others because of it.

Keys to Kingdom Living: When we love others and encourage and invest in them, we live out Proverbs 11:25: "He who refreshes others will himself be refreshed."

Doorpost: "Love one another deeply, from the heart." 1 Peter 1:22

LOVE: FOR OUR FELLOW MAN AND THE GREATER GOOD

*L*ate-night TV is filled with public service announcements of people in third world countries living in substandard conditions, with seemingly no one to love or care for them. If you're like me, there are times when your heart breaks and you stop to ponder and even act on the impulse of empathy. Other times, you hit the fast forward button on your remote or change the channel in search of entertainment to escape life's brutal realities. But hitting the remote doesn't make the problem go away or alleviate our responsibility to act as people of means and children of God.

Yet it's sometimes our inadvertent response to deceive ourselves. Thoughts like "these people aren't in my circle of influence" or "the tiny amount of help I can give won't make much of a difference" enable us to shift our thinking. Let's face it: when it comes to loving our family, our friends, and the God who made us, we can easily see that, in many ways, we have a vested interest in doing so. Even though we might genuinely love "from the heart," generally we can expect some form of reciprocity when it comes to those relationships. But what about the love we should extend to various cultures within our communities, both globally and locally? That kind of one-way love is just as important and is an integral part of being a caring, loving steward of what we have in a world of have-nots.

Jesus was continually fine-tuning His radar in search of the have-nots. Though He often worked miracles of healing, He didn't always fix or solve every illness or circumstance. But every encounter mentioned in the Bible between the Son of God and individuals who were open to Jesus Christ involves His deep love for them, and many were profoundly changed by their encounter with Him.

As Christians commissioned to share the good news of Jesus and serve as His hands and feet, we are uniquely positioned to infuse Christ-like love to the outer circles of our social sphere. When we serve meals to the homeless in our communities, pack shoeboxes filled with Christmas gifts for children overseas, or travel across the world to share the gospel with third world inhabitants in desperate need of hope, redemption, and restoration, we are obeying God's greatest commandment in the most selfless way available to us. Having these experiences myself has enabled God to open my heart to those He loves. Jesus points out in His Sermon on the Mount that "if you love those who love you, what reward will you get? Are not even the tax collectors doing that?" Of course, we don't always feel like giving, which is why Jesus says if someone else wants to "take your shirt, hand over your coat as well" (Matthew 5:40).

When it comes to selfless loving and giving, we are always in training until the day Jesus comes to take us home. We need to respond to people in need whom we don't know. Go two miles with anyone who forces us to go one. Give to the one who asks. We might not feel like it, but obedience to God always brings great reward.

Keys to Kingdom Living: Extend your love to the Earth's end, fulfilling the law of love.

Doorpost: "Do not neglect to do good and to share what you have." Hebrews 13:16 (ESV)

LOVE: COVERING A MULTITUDE
OF SINS

*T*he verse in the Bible that Peter includes about love covering a multitude of sins can be tricky to interpret. We are told countless times in Scripture that our sins are forgiven only when we repent with a contrite heart and receive God's absolution through the blood of Jesus Christ. The Message Bible clarifies it a bit. "Most of all, love each other as if your life depended on it. Love makes up for practically anything. Be quick to give a meal to the hungry, a bed to the homeless— cheerfully. Be generous with the different things God gave you, passing them around so all get in on it."

Of course, we can never cover our own sins. But by using our time, talents, and energy to love others in a Christ-like way, Peter implies here that we are called to a dual grace. It's not our love that covers our own sins. Love is the attitude that covers the wrongdoing done to us with equal measures of grace and forgiveness. Loving others places their interests at the highest level of importance. We are to think the best of others, assigning the best motives to their actions. Peter also implies that while human beings in any relationship are going to fall short and sin against each other, we need to extend grace and not make mountains out of molehills. That doesn't mean that God wasn't grieved from them or that they weren't wrong. It doesn't even mean that we were wrong in our feeling of being wronged. It just means that, in moving forward, our focus is on loving rightly rather than wrongly. We are going to need that grace as desperately as we are going to need to dispense it.

The best example of a love that covers a multitude of sins involves the inimitable love Jesus had when He died on the cross for our sins. His love covered that unimaginable multitude. His is the kind of love that is humble and noble enough to "look not only to our own interests but to the interests of others."

Often, when we are wronged, we love nothing more than to take our story walking and hold people hostage as we pour out every detail. When we choose instead to love and forgive that person, we are able to cover what they have done with the love we have *for* them, as opposed to our act of love covering our own sins.

Something else happens when we cover what's been done to us by loving the perpetrator: we liberate ourselves from feelings of injustice over something that is over and done with and perhaps no longer rectifiable. By taking this important step, we love as Christ loved us and are also positioned to receive the same kind of grace in our time of need. The longer we live, the more these weights and balances will present themselves. Will we choose to give and receive in equal measure?

Keys to Kingdom Living: God is pleased when we lovingly forgive without taking hostages.

Doorpost: "Above all, love each other deeply, because love covers over a multitude of sins." 1 Peter 4:8

ACKNOWLEDGMENTS

Many Thanks!

Above all, I am thankful to God for putting it on my heart to write this book. I never dreamed how long it would take or how many people I would need to come alongside in the process. I would like to thank, in no particular order:

Heather Manning, who was with me when the light bulb went off in my head as she told her side door story.

Community Bible Study Orange Day class leaders and students, who encouraged me, prayed for me and poured into me as mentors and friends, and to Katie Ristig in particular who faithfully read the manuscript.

To Ms. Steele, my 8th grade journalism teacher, who was the first person to encourage my writing on a paper I still have!

Barbara DeMarco Barrett, for her editing, suggestions, encouragement, and years of helping me with writing in her workshop.

Marshall Terry, my creative writing professor, who believed in me and told me I needed to devote myself to all things real in communicating and living.

Ginnie Johansen Johnson, fellow writer, who nurtured the seeds of the book and helped me be accountable to a schedule and a structure.

Lorraine Pintus, writing coach and mentor, who came

alongside with wise counsel and helped me understand writing as a ministry and a calling rather than a mere occupation.

To Pastor Tom Brashears, who walked me to the edge of the foot of the mountain with words of encouragement, a helpful book recommendation, and Bible verses for the journey.

To Kay Warren, who said she prayed for me to be brave and transparent as I wrote about pain, suffering, loss, and redemption.

My husband of 35 years, Ben Yorks, whose generosity and support both financially and otherwise helped bring these words from keyboard to paperback.

Special thanks to Jody Skinner of Every Smidgen Matters, who saw the vision for the trilogy and indeed proved invaluable regarding each and every "smidgen."

And finally, to everyone (too many to list!) who came alongside with love and support during the hard years in the room off of my side door—your kindnesses, prayers, and support have meant the world to me and I remain forever grateful. You are appreciated more than you will ever know.

Made in the USA
Columbia, SC
10 June 2019